W(

Warrior

Cecil Duckworth

ISBN HB 978-0-9570481-5-7
ISBN 978-0-9570481-4-0

A catalogue record for this book is available from the British Library

Published in Great Britain
in 2012 by
Polperro Heritage Press
Clifton-upon-Teme, Worcestershire WR6 6EN UK
www.polperro.press.co.uk

Printed by
Orphans Press
Leominster, Herefordshire
United Kingdom

Warriors are not what you think of as warriors. The warrior is not someone who fights, because no one has the right to take another life. The warrior, for us, is one who sacrifices himself for the good of others.

His task is to take care of the elderly, the defenceless, those who cannot provide for themselves, and above all, the children, the future of humanity.

Sitting Bull

Contents

For Beatrice, Mark and Jill

Foreword

I am not someone who can say I've known the author for decades. I've known of him all my adult life of course; starting out as a young corporate lawyer in Birmingham, everyone had heard of the 'owner' of Worcester Group. But I only got to know Cecil through that glorious game of rugby. I joined the board of my former clients, Leicester Tigers in 2006 and Cecil was already working his magic at Sixways. We have since had many a chat, many a shared charity initiative, many a good old grumble or a laugh.

So I came to this book in the same way as most of those who are turning these pages; I know him but don't know how he 'did it' or how he 'got there'. What lit the fire? What were the mistakes? How did it all happen? What makes one of our country's great, modest, inspiring entrepreneurs tick? And what do you do when you can have all you materially desire, when you have climbed all those personal mountains?

Dear reader, you are about to read a page-turner; a journey from which you can learn so much, from which you can take the mistakes and steal the gleaned experience and from which you can bleed the talent, the lessons, the ups and the downs and put them to work in your life, both business and personal.

'I didn't want to be Mr Average' sits with 'my second idea of developing a central heating boiler'; having 'an instinct about people' blends with bank managers of the old-school who made judgements on the person who wanted to borrow the money (legion are the small businesses today who crave a return to genuine 'people business' banking); 'evolution, a step-by-step approach' segways into 'besides, I felt we had a responsibility to export overseas'.

This book is worth ten management consultancy tomes! It's all here ... and the theory is put into practice before your very eyes. It wasn't all plain sailing. The 1973 oil crisis; the 1983 factory fire; the sheer self-destructive ideological bloody-mindedness of Liverpool pre-Thatcher trade-unionism in the seventies. But 'I always felt there would be a way out of the morass'; 'if you spend all your time worrying about the catastrophe, you probably don't concentrate on the solution'; 'instead of spending most of their time wondering if they were going to survive, they could spend all their energy doing what they were good at' and 'no, I never thought I couldn't go on, I thought we can get out of this, we can recover and I began to set about planning how we could' are pointers for us all as to how to deal with those slings and arrows of fortune.

It was Napoleon who said 'give me lucky generals' and the author has had his share of Lady Luck's benign munificence. An unreliable Jensen starts when it simply just must; a PM who is there on the necessary day; he is in the right place at the right time on many an occasion. But then (as I can attest from my own saunter through life) 'the harder you practise, the luckier you get!'

Cecil Duckworth has been a child of his time. Risk-taking at a time of pervasive socialist risk-aversion in the sixties and seventies; feeling liberated by the Thatcher revolution and making the most of it; leaving his business baby behind and diving into the unpredictable cauldron of vested interest-ridden, newly created professional rugby. It was all new for us all, it was all new for him, and this book takes you through how he turned the lot to advantage. Ever the practically-minded engineer with bucket loads of common sense, leading from the front, Cecil will (I am sure) be the first to say he couldn't have cracked it without the support, the love and the belief of Beatrice (oh! and the small matter of three hundred quid!).

But for me, the privilege of penning this foreword has been enjoyed because of two personal matters: I have believed all my life in what I call 'socially-inclusive wealth creation'. Governments should get off the backs of business and free them up to create wealth, generate tax-paying profit and sustainable employment. But the wealth creators must meet Governments half-way; they must reach out to the communities they affect by their actions, they must be there making a difference for good every day to improve communities and the quality of people's lives. I pay tribute to a man who clearly 'gets it'. Second? I said at the start that I didn't know Cecil, I knew of him. I am so very pleased that by reading this book I now know him.

Lord Digby Jones

Former Director-General of the CBI and former Minister of State for UK Trade, now UK Business Ambassador and Chairman or Advisor to many UK businesses

1

Origins

Where do ideas come from? What triggers a thought that there might be a better way of doing something? And in pursuing that thought, fulfilling the idea, is it chiefly inspiration, luck, or quiet persistence that wins out in the end?

It wasn't my idea to write about my life. I did want to get across some thoughts about being an entrepreneur, based on my experiences both in industry and rugby. And I wanted to talk about the work I have done in founding charities such as the Worcestershire Duckworth Trust. But I have no intention of sitting back in retirement. I have a great deal yet to achieve. On the other hand people said this was a good time to assess my life so far: they wanted to know what motivated me, where my ideas were formed, and that meant pausing to look at my life as a whole. It wasn't easy, because my nature is to look ahead, not to reflect on the past. However, I suppose it all began in 1937, when I was born in a village on the edge of Macclesfield in Cheshire.

Macclesfield is a friendly market town, once the centre of the silk industry. It lies in the foothills of the Pennines, east of the Cheshire plain. Today, the Peak District National Park is ten minutes' drive away. Chester is about 30 miles west, Stockport and Manchester to the north. But in the 1940s, when I was a small boy, few people had cars. The way out of that small world began at the bus stop opposite the Cock Inn across the road from our semi-detached house. There were fields behind our back garden. Milk was delivered in churns by pony and trap. We grew fruit and vegetables and kept chickens, mostly for eggs. I had my own bantam cock called Percy and my younger sister Myrtle had Jemima.

For any small boy born at that time, early life was inextricably linked to the war. My father, who had worked in a hospital in Macclesfield, was in the army and rarely home. He survived Dunkirk and was later wounded, so I have one memory of visiting him in hospital; and another seeing him in uniform at Crewe, although the really vivid imprint from that day is of the massive silver barrage balloons in a blue sky. There are other isolated images: the day a German aircraft came down a few hundred yards from the local church, just missing it, and my father being first on the scene to find the two Germans mortally wounded. Towards the end of the war a V2 rocket came down in Bluebell Wood, not far from our house. That was quite something; the V2 was the German *vergeltungswaffe 2* – retaliation weapon – and the world's first long range ballistic missile. On another occasion a friend and I walked over to the nearby airfield and a man in uniform, who I think was an officer, welcomed us and showed us round a Lancaster bomber. At the end he looked at us in sudden alarm and said you are so-and-so's son, aren't you? "No," I said cheerfully. "God," he said, "run like hell – you're not supposed to be here!" I never knew who he thought we were.

The war was simply part of life for me. I had two sisters: Sheila, who was older than me, and Myrtle. At home, we were obsessed with making sure the blackout was in place, and we slept under the stairs if the bombers came. For my parents, it probably exacerbated problems already in their marriage.

My father, Charles Duckworth, was a good-looking man, but my mother Jean was much more intelligent. I suppose she was the dominant influence, because my father was away so much in the war, although he and I shared the contents of the greenhouse – I did a good trade in selling tomatoes and cucumbers locally. My mother was from Yorkshire, and very bright, with wide interests: she loved music, books and was very keen on cricket, Len Hutton of course being a hero. The Roses games at Old Trafford between Yorkshire and Lancashire were always packed out and I remember going to watch the cricket and Manchester United with various school friends. In those days you could often get to Manchester on a platform ticket... There were holidays with my mother and two sisters in North Wales – boarding houses, and sitting on damp sand in Colwyn Bay and Rhyl. The highlights of the week being a donkey ride, a trip to a show on the pier and a knickerbocker glory.

My mother was a seamstress during the war to help make ends meet, working from home on a hand wheel sewing machine – I remember her excitement when electric sewing machines arrived. She changed from nursing to social work, and when I was about 12 or 13 she got a full time job at the local hospital. Working full time she said she would need some help with the housework on Sundays. There were three jobs, for the three of us: cleaning upstairs, cooking Sunday lunch, or cleaning downstairs. I chose cooking the Sunday lunch. We had a series of roasts, and I became a master of puddings. I made crumbles, bread and butter puddings and sponge puddings with the various fruits we grew – apples, gooseberries, blackberries. I never weighed anything, I just did it by taking so many spoons of flour, sugar, etc.

I suppose it was in those days that I showed some talent for business. I was in the Cubs, and there was a trip to Paris planned. I had to find some money for it, so I got myself a paper round to begin with. It epitomised the nature of that pleasant neighbourhood: only one *Times*, two *Manchester Guardians,* about six *Daily Telegraphs*, then the *Mail, Express, Daily Despatch* and *Daily Herald* which were in print years ago. I sold my cucumbers and tomatoes to people with long drives. On mornings when I was running late it was tempting to slip over or through a fence so avoiding going up and down those long drives. I hoped not to be seen and, as far as I know, I wasn't and I always got a Christmas tip. One family gave me 5/- (25p) which in today's money would be £5.60. I earned 7/6p a week (£9.00). Getting up early was not my thing (it still isn't!) and when it was raining it was hard work, particularly on Thursdays when the *Radio Times* made the bag heavy and difficult as the bags were not waterproofed so if the papers got wet it was not easy getting them into the letter box without ripping the paper.

My sister Myrtle fell in love with the horses owned by one such family, and still has a horse today. There was a farm close by, too, so I managed to get a Saturday job there, driving the tractor and helping with the animals and harvest. I saved up enough money and had a great time in Paris. Two things I remembered from the trip, one going around the Louvre and the other was playing football. We had been told to take our football boots and we played on a cinder pitch and to this day I'm staggered the African boys played in bare feet. They were very good too.

It was, in most ways, a happy childhood. My first school was Broken Cross Primary, and on my first day I sat next to John Cornford who became a life time friend. We both have memories of a much taller boy called Vincent who became our protector and made sure we were both looked after. It was 1942 and I remember the air raid sirens going off from time to time and we would all assemble in the air raid shelters and sing *Ten Green Bottles* and *One Man Went To Mow.* John and I grew up together and as boys we played football and cricket and since have played a lot of golf. He was my Best Man and we have had many holidays, golfing trips and family holidays with our wives and children. Later on we were in business together which proved to be very successful.

When I was about eight I met another boy called Peter Holland, who again became a life long friend. Peter was an outstanding sports player: a very good table tennis player, tennis and squash player and a pretty good cricketer, he was also a good footballer and excelled at rugby. Indeed it was he who stimulated my interest in rugby. His wife, Janet, was also to play an important role in my business life.

Peter, John and I plus a number of other good friends who I still see from time to time grew up together. We had a great time but looking back I wish I'd worked harder at school. I was moderately good at sport, captain of both football and cricket teams and I also won the 100 and 200 yards races. I left school at 16, not really sure what I was going to do. Because I was good at maths someone suggested accountancy.

I joined an accountancy firm in Macclesfield, Mellor Snape & Co where I was paid 35 shillings a week. Very quickly I could see that the partners there were earning much more money than those who weren't qualified. It was obvious, therefore, that if I was going to get anywhere I had to get qualified. There was one guy in particular I recall who was very bright but hopeless when it came to the actual exam and he didn't get qualified. I could see how big the difference was; he got all the lousy jobs and was always broke. But getting qualified was a problem for me. In the early 1950s the only way to qualify as an accountant in Macclesfield was to take a correspondence course, which I did. But a correspondence course takes an immense amount of self-discipline. If it was a sunny evening I would rather be playing cricket. It's also a lonely business. There was another factor, too. My parents' marriage was breaking up. My father was more and more difficult with my mother so it was not the best environment in which to study.

Gradually I realised that I was slipping so far behind with my studying that I didn't think I could catch up and eventually came to the conclusion that a correspondence course was not for me. I told my mother I wasn't sure I'd got the ability to get qualified. It was a traumatic moment. I realised I might end up like the guy who never passed his accountancy exams, in a reasonable position but never getting any further. And that wasn't for me. I wanted the opportunity to be one of the top people. I didn't want to be Mr Average.

At that time both my sisters were working; Sheila had just been transferred from Macclesfield to Worcester, some 100 miles south. My mother said: "I think I ought to take you away from this environment". So she and I got the train to Worcester, where I could stay with Sheila in her digs. I had a friend who told me I could get a degree-equivalent qualification by taking an HND (Higher National Diploma) in mechanical engineering, and go on to become a chartered engineer. As I was good at maths, engineering suddenly seemed a possible answer to getting into a profession where I could get a qualification. I managed to get a five-year apprenticeship with a Worcester company called Redman Engineering, which would allow me to study at the same time with day release and night school. In 1953 only 5% of school leavers went to University.

Redman's had moved from Surrey to Worcester after the war where they had a factory at Gregory's Bank in the city and was one of the leaders in manufacturing punch presses, machines used throughout industry for forming shapes or cutting holes in sheet metal, in Redman's case chiefly for the motor industry. Later it was to become part of the engineering group Redman Heenan Froude. Heenan and Froude (famous for building Blackpool Tower) were also leading designers and manufacturers of dynamometers (devices used in engineering for measuring torque and power characteristics of machines).

It was a new beginning, not only for me but for my mother who had said simply that she "had to get out". She took a job as matron at a nursing home in Stourbridge, about 25 miles from Worcester, where she could be central to our lives. We lost all contact with my father, something I was never comfortable with and years later I went to see him. It was an emotional meeting. He had got his life together and although I told him I had started my own business, he never came to Worcester to see how I was doing which, to this day, I find extremely... disappointing.

I was in a new city where I knew no one except my sister Sheila. It was lonely at first and I missed my friends. I was earning £5 a week but that didn't go far after paying rent and the suddenly apparent necessities of living: having to buy boot polish, shaving cream, razor blades, etc. which were all provided when I lived at home. But my main motivation was to become a qualified engineer. At the time I hadn't given any thought of starting up my own business. I had no distractions and I had become very disciplined and focused on passing exams.

2

Finding My Feet

I worked in the factory at Redman Engineering before moving to the drawing office, and from the beginning I could see how things might be run better - including the organisation of the tea break. No one had run it properly and it was always in debt so I said I'd have a go. I promised everybody tea every day for 1s 6d a week, and a bonus at Christmas. They all got their tea and their Christmas bonus and there was even a little left for me, which I thought was justified. Maybe this was the sowing of a seed that led me to believe I could be successful running my own business - small beginnings.

I began to get very frustrated with Redman's. Once I was in the design office I realised how conservative they were. In many ways they weren't at all progressive. Back then, in the late 1950s, the individual punch presses which they produced had to be positioned to produce a single panel with all the apertures and shapes in the right places. The product range had grown like Topsy over the years and I could see a way to eliminate all the problems that resulted from this approach so I put my ideas to my manager, and showed him the work I'd done on making a smaller, more efficient range of machines which were far better than the competition. I said we should do it, because if we didn't someone else would, and if we went ahead, people would move to the new design and it would advance the business. He looked at me and said: "You young men, you think you know everything, all these bright ideas... It would be a lot of work, you know." I didn't pursue it. I just thought, one day I'll be in competition with you. Apart from that, I'd come to the conclusion I could do it even better and use the new technology, which would change everything. Looking back, it was the germination of another idea which was developing in my mind to run my own business.

I was finding my feet in Worcester. I moved into digs in Wylds Lane and the only sad moment was when I had realised I couldn't keep our family dog, a Corgi-cross I'd brought with me from Macclesfield, but my landlord and landlady didn't want a dog around. He was only about six years old but I had to take him to the vet to be put to sleep. It was practical, but very upsetting.

My landlady ran her life with little cans of money, with labels on like 'electricity', 'gas', etc. I could always tell which day it was by what we were eating – baked beans meant Monday; Friday was always fish and chips. It was a routine I got used to. They had a television and I watched it occasionally, but I spent a lot of time in my bedroom and I went to college and joined a badminton club where I began to make friends. When I was 19 I bought my first car for £25, a 1932 Austin 10. It had a starting handle, no heating and I had to use hand signals and double declutch, but I was suddenly independent – and I could offer a lift to a girl. I parked it on some waste ground opposite my digs, to which someone objected, and threw eggs at its honeycomb radiator. I tried many times to catch him at it, but never did, and the car always smelt of eggs.

I'd learned to drive during the Suez crisis in 1956, when testing had been suspended due to the shortage of petrol, and so one didn't need a full licence, but driving tests were resumed the following year. I thought there would be a big backlog so I put in for one immediately, only to find I was booked in two weeks later. I was well aware that I had developed a lot of bad habits, like coasting round corners, hand signalling, double declutching and slipping into gear and the Austin 10 wasn't exactly examiner-friendly either. I decided I'd try and get the starter motor to work so spent a lot of time on it over the weekend before I was to take my test. It worked but only for certain when the engine was nice and hot. I drove around beforehand so that I arrived on time at the examiner's office, only to find I was asked to wait because he had to take a telephone call. The examiner took some time, during which the Austin 10 was rapidly cooling, and when he finally got into it and pressed the starter button nothing happened. I got out and used the starting handle. He was a grumpy old sod: when it came to the emergency stop he said he would drop his book on his knee, but I stopped so suddenly that his head hit the windscreen. He failed me. But I passed next time.

I wasn't a rugby player because I was too light, and my best sport was probably badminton, but I played a bit of cricket at Redman's. I remember we played St George's Laundry and bowled them out for nought, followed by me opening the batting and my partner hitting the first ball for four.

Although I was working hard for my HND, on Saturday nights I and a group of friends often used to go for a drink in the Raven Hotel in Droitwich, and then on to the Winter Gardens for a dance, hopefully to meet a nice young girl. On one such Saturday evening I looked across the crowded dance floor at the Winter Gardens and thought: that's a nice girl. I was 20 then, and she was 19. I had my Austin 10 and I could offer her a lift home. We were married four years later.

Beatrice was a local girl. She went to Worcester Girls' Grammar School, then secretarial college, working first for Lloyds Bank and then as secretary to the chief accountant at Metal Box. She had a great many friends, especially in rugby and rowing, and I took up rowing. We'd spend most Saturdays at rugby matches in the winter, and go to regattas in the summer. Eventually we won at Mumbles on the Gower Coast – in the sea. It was a coxed four scull and I was stroke. We hit the pier once but we still won, chiefly because our opposition was laughing so much at us that they drifted out to sea.

I had learned some self-discipline by then, and it was easier because life had become more settled. Two or three times a week I studied in the quietness of the city library from seven until 9.30pm, when Beatrice used to come down and we'd go to the Crown pub in Broad Street in the centre of Worcester and meet up with friends. I remember we used to play spoof, a guessing game where each player has to guess the cumulative amount of coins held: you could have none, one, two or a maximum of three. It was great fun and the loser had to buy the next round.

One of our group was the manager at Currys where the new Hoover Keymatic washing machine had just come on the market and was being advertised on television by suggesting you could go to the zoo for the day and return to find your clothing washed. A lady had come in to Currys to complain that her Keymatic wouldn't go through the programme, so our manager friend said, well, if the timer sticks, the thing to do is to give it a knock with your hand on the side of the machine... She replied in astonishment: "My dear fellow, I can't do that, I'm at the zoo!" Those evenings were part of a regular routine. Sometimes we'd push the boat out and have fish and chips...

I finally got my HND in 1960. It was a defining moment. National Service was close to coming to an end, but no one really knew when. I thought I might move out of Worcester and go to London; I even applied for a couple of jobs. But the necessity of doing National Service made employers rather less enthusiastic to take on someone who would be leaving for two years. If

I had taken one of those jobs and had a deferment from National Service I might never have started my own business.

As it was, I decided to join the RAF and sign up for three years rather than the required two for National Service. I did consider becoming a pilot, but that meant five years – too long. Whereas for three years I would be paid much more than if I'd only signed up for two, and I was allowed to have a day and a half off a week so I could finish my education and become a Chartered Engineer. And I wanted to work on my idea for a self-service petrol pump.

I was sent to Melksham in Wiltshire at first, working on instruments and radar as a Junior Technician. Short term commissions were no longer offered because the future of National Service was uncertain; I was one of the last to do it. The whole thing was running down. There were no wars, and defence cuts were in prospect. For me, the RAF meant time to think, time to plan. When I was posted to Little Rissington in the Cotswolds, I was given two days off per week to go to Cheltenham College to study to become a chartered engineer. And although I did not need to, I also studied advanced mathematics which I really enjoyed and successfully passed.

Whilst in Cheltenham I made a number of visits to the Patent Office where I took out my first patent for a self-service petrol pump. I approached a number of petrol pump manufacturers with the idea, but it was obviously going to be a long term project – they all said it would come, but I was ten years too early. I didn't get any offers of help to build a prototype so I decided to put the project on the back burner and concentrate on my second idea of developing a central heating boiler.

Houses had been heated by a form of central heating since Roman times, but it needed to be installed when the house was built. Progress had been limited. There were two systems, hot air distributed via ducts or hot water which flowed through large diameter pipes and cumbersome radiators. The big breakthrough came with the introduction of a small, high powered circulating pump, which meant 15 or 22mm pipes could be used to make the retro fitting of central heating possible. The market began to open up. The gas industry was not proactive at the time, but the oil companies, Shell and BP, decided that there was a future in oil central heating, particularly in larger houses in the more rural areas where there was room to put in an oil tank and have access to fill it. Nevertheless gas looked like being the future for houses in towns and cities, particularly once North Sea gas came on stream, which was why the major manufacturing companies decided to focus on gas.

Looking back, I liked the idea of joining an industry that was in its infancy. It had started, but it hadn't developed. I believed I could make a boiler as good as anyone else. And when I looked at the Japanese attack on our motorcycle industry, with Norton and BSA disappearing, as well as the entrance of Japanese car makers, it struck me that the heating industry was different and was not likely to face a similar attack. The housing stock and climatic conditions in Japan were not like ours. As far as I knew there was little or no competition from Europe either. If I was to do a 'me too', making something similar to the big companies, the only way to break into the market was to leapfrog them by changing the market. If they were going to forget about oil and concentrate on gas, then I would concentrate on oil and become very, very good at it. Besides, for the foreseeable future there were going to be people in rural areas and on the edge of towns who would need oil. Oil didn't need a cast iron boiler: it could be manufactured out of steel. A fabricated boiler. And North Sea gas, when it came in, would work perfectly well with a fabricated boiler. The idea of a strategy was evolving.

I had talked to Beatrice about my ideas, of course. About starting my own business when I left the RAF. She had always been encouraged by her mother to put money by, and she had saved £300. She said she would give it to me to help start the business. It was Beatrice's gift that founded the company.

One weekend, back in Worcester, I met up with a group of friends in the pub and I was talking about what I wanted to do. A friend of mine, Ken Hamilton, who was going out with a close friend of Beatrice's at the time, was listening. Ken had a law degree and was completing his accountancy exams. He said: "You thinking of starting your own business? Interested in me joining you?" I said, "Well, if you've got £300 you can!" I thought, well, he's an accountant with a law degree, I'm an engineer; why not? I was a bit naïve in those days. We discussed the name of the company. 'Duckworth and Hamilton' was a bit of a mouthful. I remembered a company called Cincinatti Engineering, and I liked the idea of identifying with the town where something was made. So Worcester Engineering was born.

I enjoyed my time in the RAF. We were tested every week and there was quite a bit of rivalry between us all. Some of us had A levels or had been to independent schools, and I realised then that I could hold my own with these guys. Most nights on the station we played squash or badminton – I played badminton for the station and the Command, and I think it has probably been my best sport. In the evenings we played a card game called Solo. It was developed from a Spanish game, Hombre, based on English whist, and it involves trick-taking, with four players. It's the ideal background to playing bridge, which is now one of my passions.

There was another reason life was good then. Beatrice and I became engaged. We set the wedding date for September in 1961, but there was a slight interruption when President Abdul Karim Kassem of Iraq, following Kuwait's independence, decided to make a claim to that country. He declared that Kuwait had been part of the Ottoman Empire and was therefore subject to Iraqi sovereignty. In June the Emir of Kuwait requested assistance from the Saudi Arabian and British governments, and Britain quickly deployed troops, aircraft and ships to the area. So I found myself on my way to Bahrain as part of Operation Vantage. I went out there with a friend called Arthur Money, working on the instrumentation of aircraft. It was a time when gunboat diplomacy really worked: after six weeks Iraq decided it didn't want Kuwait after all. The RAF used to buzz Baghdad several times a day which proved very effective. Perhaps that episode has some relevance today. Afterwards we were all given six weeks off in gratitude for our efforts, and I turned my mind to how I was going to afford a decent honeymoon.

It was a very hot summer. The M5 motorway was being built, and I discovered they were looking for engineers. One had just rolled his Land Rover and the project engineer was pretty desperate. I went for the job, and got it, just like that – he didn't even ask me what kind of engineer I was, which was lucky, because I was a mechanical, not a civil engineer. Nor did I tell him that I was still in the RAF. I might have known nothing about the job, but my team did, and in any case it was not difficult, anyone could have done it. We had to take soil samples where they were building bridges, then bake the sample, do a compression test and record the results. It was data to be held in case of future problems with cracking, that sort of thing. I made enough money for the honeymoon, but when I told the project engineer I'd been 'recalled' to the RAF he wasn't too pleased. I now tell people I built the M5 which is not quite true, but the motorway is still in good order 50 years later.

Beatrice and I were married in Worcester and went to the Costa Brava for our honeymoon, which was very picturesque and very unspoilt then. We rented half a cottage in Milton-under-Wychwood, a lovely little village near Little Rissington. We used to go into Burford for the odd meal. Most days I got a lift in with Arthur Money, so that Beatrice could have the Austin 10. Sometimes I wonder how she drove it. It was a very happy time.

I left the RAF in 1962. I had £300 capital, a patent, and a lot of self belief. And I had two ideas. Could I get one or both to work? It was the beginning.

3

The Firefly

Worcester once led the world in vinegar production. Founded in 1830 by two local chemists, William Hill and Edward Evans, Hill Evans & Co was the biggest vinegar works of its kind in the world. It also had the world's largest vat, 40 feet high with a capacity of well over nearly 115,000 gallons. By the early twentieth century it was producing two million gallons of malt vinegar a year. Its six acres of massive red brick buildings at Lowesmoor in the St Martins Gate area of the city were linked to the railway by a dedicated branch line to Shrub Hill. The vinegar works finally closed in 1965 and today the agglomeration of handsome Victorian buildings has been considerably culled, and Lowesmoor is undergoing a major redevelopment. When I went to take a look at one of the then empty buildings, the factory was already in sharp decline, but I needed a thousand square feet for Worcester Engineering. I couldn't afford to worry about the fact that the building was cold, damp, low-ceilinged and undecorated, and had no three-phase electricity.

A large quantity of thick black cabling solved the electricity problem, although it took some handling to fasten it along the brick wall and into a junction box inside. Winter was coming on and we found a contraption we called Puffing Billy to provide the heating. It was about five feet tall with a chimney and a bowl of fuel oil in the base. It took a bit of lighting but once alight, it kicked out a lot of heat. It was very dangerous of course, and if we had knocked it over – as well we might, moving around in a pretty confined area – it would have caused the biggest fire in Worcestershire. However, we survived.

Then there was the bank to approach. I was with NatWest, but I didn't want all my eggs in one basket, and Ken Hamilton suggested I try his bank, Barclays. The bank manager was one of the old fashioned kind: a very nice old gentleman called Colonel Cronin. Bank managers in those days had authority. I told him what I was going to do, and of my ideas for the self-service petrol pump and the boiler. I realised as I spoke that it sounded very speculative, depending as it did on short-term funding through sub-contracted work from my old company. But I remember his exact words: "Well, I'm going to back you. I like what you've proposed, and I'll lend you a thousand pounds". That would be more than £15,000 today.

We were on the way, but to fund the work on the boiler and the petrol pump I had to expand our sub-contract work. I already had a contract with Redman's to grind carbon tips, high carbon blades used in the punch pressing process, and I'd bought a cutter grinder. I designed a jig and took on my first employee, Harold Cushway, who was able to work in the evenings part-time. That was just about keeping the wolf from the door, but I decided to invest in a metal flame-cutting piece of equipment, and a secondhand set of rolls. They were what I needed to make a boiler: but they might, I thought, be useful to someone else. I didn't enjoy touting for business, nor was it very productive. And occasionally I found myself in some odd situations.

One company in Droitwich, a small engineering business, agreed to see me. I was invited into the office by a director, and I noticed a television in the corner was showing the racing from Wincanton. Before I could start my pitch the chap said he just wanted to wait and see if his horse came in – which indeed it did. Then the telephone rang. He spent a few minutes talking to someone at the other end about a large contract due to come through, for 'thousands', and suggested he add sixpence to the price of which the person on the other end of the line would get threepence, and he would collect the other. Perhaps I was a bit of an innocent, but I wondered what was going on. If it was what I thought it was, it was a world I didn't want to enter. I went back to the Old Vinegar Works and told Harold Cushway about it. He said, "Did he show you the racing? And have a conversation about adding on a few pence per item? Well, the horse race is a recording, and there was no one at the other end of the telephone line. That's what he always does. Don't touch him". I was learning.

Nevertheless I met some honest people, and not just honest but generous and imaginative. Among them were an engineer and buyer from Morgan Crucible, who had been making crucibles and furnaces used in industrial processes since 1856. Crucibles are containers used to melt and carry metals within a furnace and in a vast range of industrial processes. The essentials of the furnace are the same as those of a domestic boiler, and in North America the word furnace is more commonly used, but Morgan Crucible were making furnaces for industry. Nevertheless, from our point of view, they were an ideal fit with our boiler project: our flame cutting machine could cut the metal, our rolling machines could roll the cylinders. Despite the fact we had actually made only one prototype boiler at this stage, the people at Morgan Crucible must have been convinced, because they placed an order for 30 furnaces.

With the sub contracting now under way I could concentrate on the boiler. I had been in touch with a burner manufacturer, Langdons of Staines, who made burners under licence from the United States, and I was warmly welcomed by Mr Langdon himself. He was ex-RAF, with a lot of charm, and very generous in giving us technical assistance – because, as he said, he wanted to sell burners. They gave me a lot of information and let me look at their test rigs; armed with their help I went back to perfect our boiler. We had to think of a name for it, and because the burner had a rotor in the centre which spun the oil out in a fine spray which was then ignited by the electric spark – we decided on Firefly, which was later to seem a little ironic.

It was a busy time. I designed a test rig for the boiler: testing was vital in getting to the level of efficiency we wanted. There was no official testing house at that time for oil fired central heating, but Shell and BP were keen to promote oil as a fuel and were therefore interested in recommending reliable oil fired boilers. They were then operating a joint marketing strategy, and if you could convince their engineers that your boiler was efficient and reliable you were on your way. They would send the engineers to test the boiler and, if satisfied, approve it for use with their oil.

A boiler is essentially a double-skinned cylinder with a gas or oil burner on top or at the bottom. That's the business end, where the oil is mixed with air and burned to provide the heat. Heat is transferred to the water via the heat exchanger through which water flows. The water is thereby heated, and although there will be a convection current set up as it gets hotter, a circulating pump speeds up the flow.

I was always trying to improve the design and its manufacture. For example, rather than flame-cutting out the metal ring at the top of the boiler with an oxy-acetylene cutter, I designed a system of rollers to bend the sheet of metal which would form the inner and outer skins of the cylinder. There had always been problems with the metal distorting in the heat of the flame-cutter, and the edges of the metal being rough, which made welding the top of the boiler more difficult, and this way we eliminated those problems. We altered the rollers by putting grooves in them, and then hardened pads to protect the rollers from wearing. I remember watching the first time that the metal went through the rollers. It was hugely satisfying to see that it worked as intended. This would save about an hour's production time, save metal and be a far superior job. Similarly, at another stage, when we heard from installers that corrosion was a problem because the cold water coming into the boiler impinged directly on the inner skin, I realised that if we put in a small mild steel baffle to make the cold water mix with the hot water as it came in, we could avoid the problem. We fitted the baffle on every boiler and we never had a cold water corrosion problem. Such evolutionary and empirical ideas not only worked, but also saved us hundreds of thousands of pounds.

One problem with fabricated boilers was that they could leak if there was a tiny pinhole in the welding process. Our number one tester, Gerald Bowen, tested thousands of boilers. At the outset I promised him one shilling for every one he tested, but if one leaked he would pay me £5. He was a fantastic worker and extremely diligent. He also set a wonderful example. He would always be ready to start work at 8am and on the stroke of eight he would start banging away. He was the same at the tea break. He would work right up to the time the buzzer went and then start immediately when the buzzer went again ten minutes later. We also employed his brother Reg, his wife Sheila and their son Rick. They, and a lot of our workers, were magnificent and I believe I could not have found better workers anywhere in the world. They helped me build a successful business. If a boiler was returned reportedly leaking, Gerald would shake his head, put the boiler on test at twice the pressure of the normal test and prove that it didn't leak. I had to believe him and never recovered one £5 penalty.

While working on the boiler we were also cutter-grinding and building furnaces for Morgan Crucible. Evenings were a hive of activity at the Old Vinegar Works, with more part-time evening workers, including Percy Jones a welder who owned some property in Worcester and who became an important part of the company. One of his sons still works for the company today.

Beatrice was involved then, too. Not only did she do all the invoicing once a month, staying up late on Sunday evenings, but often came to the works to answer telephone calls. That didn't last very long, because our son Mark was born in 1962. Mark had some problems and Beatrice had her hands full. Four years later we had a daughter, Jill. At that time we were living in a flat in the Brickfields area of Worcester, and I was always determined to live no more than 15 minutes away from the works, so that I could get home for lunch and to help at bath time. I became happily familiar with lunchtime children's television – Parsley the Lion was my favourite, but *The Pogles* were particularly good. I would go back to the factory in the evenings and work until about 10.15. There was then a pub across the road called the Locomotive, run by two ladies who put the towels over the pumps every evening at precisely 10.30pm, and if we were ten seconds late we didn't get a drink. Ken Hamilton, who had put his £300 into the company to match Beatrice's savings, would usually call in to see how I was doing and get a pint in for me before the ladies called time. Now that we have more relaxed drinking laws, I look back at those determined landladies at the Locomotive and wonder if they didn't have the right idea after all.

A little gang of people used to turn up at the Locomotive most evenings at about ten, among them Mick Knighton who had a workshop next to our unit. He used to build wrought iron gates and repair cars among other things. He impressed me by working 48 hours non-stop, but on the other hand he would then be absent for three days and I would find myself dealing with his customers. One of them, Martin Patrick, became a close friend. He lived in Farnham and had a small van, which was to be of considerable significance later on. Martin was often among the group of us at the Locomotive, and it was Percy Jones who suggested that we test our newly completed Firefly boiler in one of the terrace houses he owned in Worcester. The tenants, fortunately, had departed.

There are times when somehow you know you should not do something, but you do it anyway. Is it lack of experience, concentration, or simply impatience to get on with the job? Whatever the psychological quirk that makes these things happen, I set the calibration jar for the oil flow into the boiler at twice the volume it should have been, despite knowing perfectly well that the calibration was double what it appeared to be. Then we left the boiler to do its work. We returned the following day and opened the front door. There was an acrid smell of oil. That might have warned us. Also a blue haze in the air. Again, we proceeded to do precisely what we should not have done: open a window. The extra oxygen ignited the excess oil and the chimney caught fire.

Fortunately the fire brigade was swiftly on the scene, and we all set about cleaning up and repainting the house. Since I knew what had happened I was entirely calm about it. The boiler worked perfectly after that unfortunate start. Soon afterwards Shell approved the boiler. It was now decision time, and although we still had only made one boiler I went to Staines to see Mr

Langdon. It was, or so it seemed to me, a momentous occasion. My intention was to place an order for ten oil burners. The cost was not enormous – each burner cost about £30 – but I was aware that we not only had to manufacture ten boilers, but sell them. Nevertheless Mr Langdon was delighted. He took me out to lunch with two of his colleagues and introduced me to steak Diane and crêpe suzettes. I came away thinking this was not a bad way of doing business but I mustn't get carried away.

We now had to design some marketing tools: a leaflet. I happened to know an artist, Ivor Drinkwater, who had done some work for my old company, Redman's, so he and I got together in his little upstairs studio in Broad Street. I spent ages over this one leaflet, drawing my ideas from domestic appliance manufacturers while he did the artwork and got photographs taken. He also designed some business cards so that I could set off with my leaflets, my business cards and a list of Shell and BP engineers to see if I could sell that first boiler. In the early 1960s, when the central heating industry was in its infancy in this country, there was no recognised distribution system. And we were bucking the trend by bringing the boiler into the kitchen, and by necessity having to make it clean and quiet. Ivor produced an advert for our local Worcester newspaper, *Berrow's Journal*: It claimed 'Less 25 per cent on your fuel bill, sir! What's Firefly's secret? The new wonder wall flame burner, the latest, most efficient, up-to-date burner on the market, gives domestic hot water and central heating with so many advantages'. Among the advantages were 'quiet, no smells, no dirt, perfectly safe...' And before we had actually produced a boiler, other than the prototype, we sold our first one, to Mountfield's of Kidderminster.

Although most manufacturers were selling through builders' merchants at the time, I decided to sell direct to the heating engineers, which meant that I could undercut our competitors. There was a certain amount of deception, or rather, creative marketing involved; I had to convince installers that the company was large enough to handle not only sales but technical support. As I was the sole salesman, administrator and service engineer, that wasn't always easy. While the company was small, selling locally meant we could sell direct. We could also tailor-make the boiler to some extent, so I was able to offer the option of a programmer and circulating pump already fitted. Having designed the boiler, I was able to talk authoritatively about its technical merits. Again, selling locally and in small numbers gave me a huge advantage - I must have been the most informed boiler salesman in the country.

I realised pretty soon that I'd have to make a bigger boiler, which we did, and Shell approved it. Within 18 months we were outgrowing the Old Vinegar Works so we decided to move to Carden Street in Worcester, east of the Cathedral, behind what was then Fownes' glove factory. It provided us with 5,000 square feet in a new building. We knew we might have some difficulty in paying the rent and we still had problems, among them the unreliability of the enamelling of the cabinets because we had to sub-contract it to a company who put us at the bottom of their schedule. Yet, looking back, I think that was the moment when I knew we would be successful. I had had doubts at the beginning – and pushed them aside – but they had given way to confidence that Worcester Engineering would succeed. It seemed like a good time to take on our first sales representative.

I reckoned that the best area for selling our boilers was in the reasonably affluent Home Counties, and I rented a room in an Oxford hotel to interview those candidates who replied to my advertisement. I saw five, and none of them apart from the last were at all interested in seeing the works. But John Carter, who had been doing extremely well with one of our competitors, did. I warned him we were a very small company (although I got Harold Cushway and four part-timers to come in during the day and make it look as though there were rather more of us). He joined us and was immediately successful. Martin Patrick, who I had met through Mick Knighton at the Locomotive, was our delivery service – living in Farnham and working in Worcester, he would go home every Friday night with two of our boilers in the back of his van. Customers were sometimes startled to find their boilers being delivered at eight o'clock at night.

Sometimes we used British Rail to take a boiler on the train from Shrub Hill Station. If we hadn't got a vehicle to use, one of our part-timers, Walter Davis, would put the boiler on a sack truck and run - not walk - with it up to the station half a mile away.

We did buy a delivery lorry soon afterwards. It had a tail lift for handling the boilers, but we couldn't afford a box wagon: it was an Austin flatbed lorry with a green canvas top, a somewhat conspicuous vehicle, but it kept the boilers dry. I would always make sure it was safely parked outside the factory at the weekend, so I was surprised one Monday morning to receive a telephone call from the police: "Where was your wagon over the weekend?" I said it was definitely at the factory on Saturday night – but no, I wasn't sure about Sunday. "Would it surprise you, Mr Duckworth, to know that on Sunday it was in Stow on the Wold?"

Apparently one of our part-time drivers had been asked to cooperate with a theft of whisky from Kay's warehouse. The thieves had broken into Kay's, stolen the whisky and used our lorry to transport it. Since it was a very distinctive vehicle and a passer-by had taken the licence number, the gang was swiftly found and charged. I had to go to court in Stafford to confirm that the thieves had not had my permission to use the vehicle, but they pleaded guilty at the last minute. Nevertheless I stayed to watch the proceedings, and was shaken by the way the judge dismissed the defendants' mitigating circumstances: "I don't believe you found this whisky on the pavement..." The sentences seemed a trifle harsh, although the chap who got nine years did have a record. The others got six and three years. I was quite shaken by the experience and drove very slowly home.

The new factory in Carden Street was giving us the chance to expand. It was a modern unit which provided superior working conditions and without the dangers of Puffing Billy. But unfortunately it had what was to become a major problem. Whereas the Locomotive pub had called last orders sharp at 10.30pm, the landlord of the pub in Carden Street liked the company of his customers until the early hours. This was not good news. I'd have a pint around half past ten and usually get home about eleven, but it was tempting to chat on about the issues of the day – one of which was the power of the unions, of which more later – and be there until well after midnight. I was driving the company forward and I felt I had to exercise some discipline. I suggested we limit ourselves to three pints maximum, which wasn't much when you are 25. I said two would be my limit. However I heard that Ken Hamilton was often in the pub until three or four in the morning. It was the beginning of a problem that was later to surface at the worst possible time.

4

Diglis Basin

Diglis Basin, where the Worcester and Birmingham Canal finally linked up with the River Severn in 1815, is now a lively hub where boats, new apartments and cafes share the shimmer of water and willows. It was once simply an area of water meadows south of the Cathedral (the name possibly originates from the French *d'eglise*). The most notable company there was the Royal Worcester Porcelain factory to the north of the Basin, but by the early 1960s it had long been in decline, so much so that production has now stopped and the only thing left is the Museum which is well worth visiting. British Waterways then began a programme of reclamation, using silt from the dredged Severn to build up the surrounding land above the flood level. When the land became available for leasing, I was the first to put in a bid for enough land to build a new factory six times the size of the Carden Street works.

We were now profitable and the bank helped us to finance the new factory; although we had expanded rapidly by 1968, we were still comparatively small. But we needed more space. We had a production line with about 50 employees, doing everything from welding to rolling the boiler cylinders, assembling the electrics and testing – and by now we had office staff. My old friend Ken Hamilton had qualified as an accountant and joined us as finance director. In addition we had a continuing problem with enamelling, an important part of the production process that was subcontracted. Our sub-contractor gave us the quality but they were very unreliable in meeting our demand and we needed to take control by investing in an enamelling plant. At the time we did not have the capital or the space so we were in a Catch 22 situation. Our supplier just could not keep up with our demand so they were limiting our growth and we were very concerned we would become an unreliable supplier which, if it continued, would be a disaster.

We obtained sufficient land to build a 30,000 square foot factory with car parking. At the time we only needed 15,000 square feet even including an enamelling plant, but we would then be able to expand if demand continued to increase. We were the first factory in Diglis Basin, and I found myself sorting out the installation of all the necessary utilities like gas, electricity, telephone and sewerage – not my job, but I wanted to get our factory built. And I wanted it to look good, so we took trouble over the landscaping. We liked people coming to see us, and we wanted them to be impressed. I got in touch with Peter Walker, Conservative MP for Worcester, who was then in Edward Heath's shadow cabinet, and asked if he would consider opening the factory. He said he would love to do so. We had a great day and proceeded to the Diglis Hotel for post-opening refreshments. Inviting Peter Walker was to be the beginning of another lifetime friendship.

The business was now not only expanding but consolidating. We had about a dozen salesmen, all of whom had Morris Minor estates - big enough to fit a boiler in the back to demonstrate what they were selling. I had a Morris Oxford. But the salesmen all fancied something a bit flashier: Vauxhalls or Fords were very fashionable at the time so they were trying to encourage me to get something a little more adventurous so that they could upgrade theirs. Eventually I decided the business might just afford it, and I bought a secondhand Jaguar saloon – which quite quickly became a new Jaguar 2+2 E-Type. I loved it. It was probably the best car I've ever had, partly because no car can ever quite equal the car of your dreams at 30 years old. Unfortunately, a year or so later I was approaching Worcester on the M5 when the offside front tyre blew and in trying to control the car it thundered into the bank which severely damaged the front of it. For a while I wasn't sure if it would be a write-off or not. I couldn't replace it, because Jaguar had introduced a new 12 cylinder version for which there was heavy demand and meant a very long delivery time.

In 1966 Jensen Motors had started building the Jensen Interceptor (although the name had been used for an earlier car made in the 1950s). It had a steel body shell designed by Carrozzeria Touring of Italy, and an American Chrysler V8 engine. It was twice the price of an E-Type but I just loved the look of it. I did suggest to my PA that she might give Jensen a call, but although things were going pretty well I told myself I would have to forget about it, it was just too expensive. I was getting lifts home. I was without a car as the garage was assessing the cost of repairs to my E-Type. But one afternoon I was waiting outside the factory when I saw not one but two Jensen Interceptors cruising round the playing field alongside the factory. They came to a halt beside me and one of the drivers said: "Mr Duckworth? I understand you might be interested in a Jensen? We just happened to be coming this way, and wondered if you would like a look... This one is three years old, and this one only six months. Have you time for a test ride?" It was one of the best pieces of selling I've ever experienced.

The Jensen Interceptor had electric windows and a built in music cartridge with a beautiful speaker system – all new then and only available in the top of the range cars. So when it was suggested that I take Beatrice out in it over the weekend and subsequently, not having returned it by the following Tuesday, was told "Don't worry, I'm going away for a couple of days, just give me a ring next week," (I was then told the E-Type was a write off) - well, of course we did a deal. And twelve months later I bought a new one. It might have been an indulgence, but it was a great car to drive and was to prove its worth only a few years later.

Those few years, from 1968 into the early 1970s, also saw the establishment of an enduring management team. Among its members was Arthur Money, my old friend from the RAF who was working for Yorkshire Imperial Plastics and had moved to the Midlands. He was to become Technical Sales Manager with a vital role in the company. Then there was Roger Tomlinson, a disenchanted schoolteacher whom I met at a party. At the time we were having problems with cost control and getting materials in on time, partly because we were expanding so quickly, and although we had been benefiting from our increasing volumes because we could buy cheaper, inflation was beginning to make itself felt. Roger had resigned his job out of frustration and had no idea what he was going to do next. "Would you say you were an organised person?" I enquired. "Good at maths? Because if you are, I might have a job for you." It might seem a slightly *ad hoc* means of finding staff, but Roger joined us on a trial run and was, indeed, very organised. He took a half a day a week to do an MA in Birmingham, adding theory to his new learning experience, and after two years became purchasing director.

I believe I have an instinct about people. It isn't always so but on balance generally worked. Colin Brookes, who became sales manager, was another example. I used to call him my Georgie Best - at the time, an accolade – because Colin was a great character, liked and admired by everyone, with a real talent for creating rapport with those vital people, the installers, and with the rest of the sales team. He did need controlling, and he wasn't at all organised, but he had a huge personality and a way of talking that just made you smile. Sales meetings were a lot of fun: I've always believed that if you work hard you can also play hard, and we would always involve the staff in these meetings every three or four months, going on boat trips up the River Severn and enjoying a get together and a meal.

It was Colin who, at a trade exhibition in London at which, for once, we didn't have a stand of our own, persuaded the people running the PA system to let him take over. Strolling down one of the aisles I suddenly heard him announcing: "Good morning everybody, I'm Colin Brookes from Worcester Engineering and hope to see you on the Shell stand – and I just thought I ought to explain why we're not here exhibiting today..." He carried on like this for a considerable time and I suspect there was a lot of fury among other exhibitors, but he even managed another broadcast later on. As he was hopeless at paperwork, I gave him a little cassette recorder so he could send a tape in to the office. Listening to it in the car, as I invariably did, I would find myself laughing out loud at his additions to the facts.

He mentioned casually to me one day that he felt he ought to tell me that he was up in court on the following Thursday, and when I asked why, he said, "Well, it's GBH". He proceeded to tell me the circumstances at some length, as was his way: "Well, I was in a bar, and I waited, and I asked for a pint of bitter, please, and the barman took no notice of me. Then a gentleman came alongside me. The barman came back and looked at him, not at me, and took his order, so I said again, 'pint of bitter please'. He took no notice of me again. I wanted to alert him to my requirements, and as there happened to be some meat pies on my side of the bar, I took one of these pies and flung it at him. It hit him on the ear. I repeated, 'PINT OF BITTER, PLEASE!' At which point he called the police and they arrested me." As I remember, he got away with a warning and a small fine.

Unfortunately Colin built up a bit of a relationship with a local girl and I used to find him drifting back to Worcester a little too often, so I had to let him know that wasn't on. He didn't stay with us and was replaced as sales manager by David Jones, another very successful salesman who had joined us a few years earlier and who was to become sales director. He was another great character and did not take as much controlling as Colin.

Selling is crucial, but I never let the salesmen have control over deals. I controlled deals. My view was that we should back sell: in other words, create the market for our boiler through the heating engineers. Selling a domestic appliance like a television, mobile phone or a vacuum cleaner is totally different. Their manufacturers can create a market by advertising their products directly to the general public. We could do the same to some extent, but the significant difference was that a boiler had to be installed by a qualified heating engineer.

A central heating boiler isn't a stand-alone product. It cannot just be taken home and plugged in. If the heating engineer wasn't convinced that a Worcester boiler was as good as we said it was, he would not recommend it and the customer would not get to hear about the product. Our job was to win over the heating engineer and convince him that not only was our boiler better than anyone else's but we could also give him technical support, impress upon him how simple it was to install and reassure him that if there was a problem we would ensure that the householder wasn't left high and dry.

Sometimes we were called out because of installation problems or the householder simply had not read the operating instructions. It is costly to provide this service but our marketing strategy was that we are not selling just a boiler but a package which could justify the price of the boiler. This package was to provide the most technically advanced compact boiler, reliable, stylish and easy for the householder to operate. For the engineer – to provide training, technical support, ease of installation and after sales service. The engineer had recommended our boiler so it was vital that he was convinced it was the best boiler available, it was value for money and knew that if the householder needed support we could provide it quickly and efficiently.

We specialised in trade evenings, when we would invite 50 to 100 engineers to watch a demonstration of how the boiler worked. Our objective was to convince the installer that we were providing the best boiler that money could buy so that he could recommend our boiler and know he was going to have a satisfied customer who would recommend him to their friends. One of the advantages of those trade evenings was that it was a two way process. We listened to the installers, and learnt a lot because they would know the problems. Often, when I was driving home or some time later, the solution would come to me. In the factory I carried out the same policy; someone might say, "I could do this job in half the time if I had x, y or z..." and sometimes I had to quietly point out that was not so, but sometimes I thought, that's a good idea, and I could introduce change quite rapidly as a result of that brief dialogue. It was a part of being intimately involved with every stage of the business and having rapport with the workforce.

Producing a domestic appliance meant having to think about the customer in their kitchen; also the heating engineer who needs it to be made easy for him to install; the maintenance engineer who has to service the boiler

– and then, how can you make it economical enough to compete in the marketplace? It's all about design and production engineering – to be as efficient as you can make it and competitive in every aspect. Then you can market that advantage to beat the competition. It's exciting and challenging. Competition is the last thing you want but it's a great driver for you to work hard to ensure the boiler is superior. Selling direct to the heating engineer enabled us to undercut the price of our competitors who sold through builders' merchants. In the early 1960s we were still only a small company and the merchants didn't want to stock another oil-fired boiler. As a result I thought that we should set up our own distribution network. They would be specialist heating distribution companies not only selling Worcester oil-fired boilers but all the other components that go into a heating system. We advertised in Macclesfield, my home town, and got a very good applicant, Arthur Lawrance, from nearby Stockport. He agreed to set up the company for us which was the start of Cheshire Heating Supplies. Arthur quickly rented a warehouse and was buying equipment and selling it the following day. He knew what to buy and he knew his customers so he was immediately successful. We did advertise in other areas of the country but never found another Arthur Lawrance.

To set up Cheshire Heating Supplies, I had needed a loan from the bank. I thought it would be good to have a different bank to Barclays, who were our main bankers. It made sense to keep things separate. So I went to NatWest, my own bank. The manager was not dissimilar to Colonel Cronin, who had given me my first loan: Vic Carter was an old fashioned manager, ex-RAF, and once again supported me and became a very good friend. In fact it was Vic who saved the day, but more about this later.

By the late 1960s our Firefly Worcester boilers were selling very well. We had established a market for our products so local merchant, OBC, wanted to stock our products. I thought it was time to review our policy of selling direct and setting up a string of distributors like Cheshire Heating Supplies. As a result I went to see Wolseley-Hughes at their headquarters in Droitwich, only seven miles from Worcester.

Wolseley-Hughes had an interesting history. Founded in Australia in 1887 by an Irishman, Fred Wolseley, it began by producing a sheep-shearing machine. Herbert Austin joined the company in 1888, and by the turn of the century it had moved to Birmingham and diversified into bicycles and cars. The first Wolseley appeared in 1896 costing £119 (with an initial production run of one, like ours). Herbert Austin then left to set up his own empire at

Longbridge, while the original Wolseley Sheep Shearing Machine company merged with Geoffrey H. Hughes, a Birmingham manufacturer of wheels, to become Wolseley-Hughes. In 1960 it bought a heating company, Nu-Way Heating. There was subsequently a little local difficulty with a somewhat 'interesting' character called Fred Evans who was a trade unionist. To keep him occupied and out of trouble he was given the job of looking after spares – oil burning components. Hence the name: OBC.

The main board of Wolseley-Hughes became aware that people were beginning to ask for more than simply basic spare parts. They wanted boilers, circulating pumps, radiators, cylinders, etc. Suddenly, by accident, the director realised it was possibly the start of a new business with huge potential. Two more companies in the field were acquired and added to what had once been a sideline to OBC and went on to become the largest heating and building supply companies in the world. They became aware of us as they were fast building up their branch network across the country – I suspect we were something of a nuisance because we were selling direct to heating engineers. We were local to their head office in Droitwich so I met the three directors, Jeremy Lancaster, John Footman and John Chislett. They were very impressive and understood the warehousing business, the logistics and stock controls. They also had developed a comprehensive computerised package which was very new in those days, far in advance of anything else I'd seen. I was impressed and quickly came to the conclusion they would be a great company to work with. Direct selling had worked for us but to have our products stocked in their ever-increasing local branch network would be a tremendous advantage. We agreed terms, ended our policy of selling direct and that was the start of a very successful and enduring partnership. If we could have developed a network of successful outlets like Cheshire Heating then that would have been different. But we would then be in direct competition with Wolseley who had become very successful and extremely professional.

What we had to ensure was that we controlled the marketing of our products. I always remember going round a warehouse with a purchasing manager at one of the builders' merchants. All around were our boilers in their cardboard boxes, and he kept referring to them simply as 'cardboard boxes', not as boilers. I thought about all the effort we'd put in, all the skill and attention to detail we had put into the production of the boiler inside that cardboard box. He may not care which boiler was inside, but we did. To ensure it was a Worcester boiler we had to create the demand for our product. The merchant would then stock our product and deliver it to the heating engineer. That had to be the process if we were going to be profitable.

Wolseley-Hughes bought Yorkshire Heating and moved their headquarters to Ripon. John Footman became Managing Director. John Chislett moved to the USA to head up a very successful operation and Jeremy Lancaster became Chairman and remained at the Group HQ in Droitwich. They were a great team and became personal friends.

I kept Cheshire Heating Supplies on a low profile, although it was sometimes mentioned with a certain suspicion. I'd assure them that there was probably going to be a management buyout and anyway OBC were getting better terms. They lived with that. And Cheshire Heating Supplies not only continued to flourish, but was to play an important part in our future - in a very significant way.

Within three years of the opening of the new factory at Diglis Basin, I realised our increased sales were such that we needed to double its size, as originally envisaged. We also wanted to add extra offices and a showroom so that we could demonstrate our products to installers. I approached Barclays, but Colonel Cronin had by then retired and the new manager, Ted Farrell, felt we were expanding too quickly and would not lend us the money to expand. I went back to see Vic Carter at NatWest, who was handling Cheshire Heating Supplies for us. Within 24 hours he said he would back us. I returned to Barclays and told Ted Farrell that we were going ahead anyway and if they wanted to help I wanted a definite answer within 24 hours. I didn't get a definitive answer so we changed banks. Ted Farrell didn't agree with me, but on reflection it was one of the good decisions I made. Within a few short years Vic Carter was to play a vital part in our very survival.

Not that there was any premonition of disaster in 1970, although there was a family tragedy. My elder sister Sheila died suddenly after a very short illness, probably CJD. She was only in her late 30s and left a young son, Paul. It was all very tragic and upsetting and I still think of Sheila very fondly.

Otherwise it was a good year. The new factory extension in Diglis Basin was completed. For the second time Peter Walker, now in government as Secretary of State for the Environment, came to open it. At the time he was regarded as a potential leader of the Conservative party and he was a wonderful speaker. He arrived in his Bentley with his new wife, Tessa, and showed no inclination to disappear after the opening. He was genuinely interested in what we were doing and the development of the company. We had come a long way since he had opened the first phase of the factory in 1968; although we were still relatively small, employing about 80 people, we had a turnover of £500,000 and had overtaken Potterton who had been the market leader in sales of domestic oil-fired boilers. Peter Walker invited Beatrice and I for dinner. It was the start of a lifelong friendship and Peter played a significant role in the future of the company.

It was also the year we moved house. We had seen an old farmhouse for sale with 13 acres of land overlooking the Malvern Hills. It was 1½ miles away from the village of Kempsey on top of a small hill near Worcester and only about 150 yards from 100 acres of common land. It had six stables, a granary and a couple of old barns. I sketched out some rough plans which included a sizeable extension, a large double garage and an indoor swimming pool. The orientation of the house was very important to Beatrice so the kitchen was moved so that it would receive the morning sun. The company was going well but I had very little personal wealth so I got a friend to draw up the plans and organised the work to be sub-contracted. I remember telling my friend when drawing up the plans to ensure the garage was deep enough to house a Rolls Royce. It was a family joke at the time but although I have not owned a Rolls Royce yet, I have had a number of Bentleys.

About this time I met Jeremy Eckersley who introduced me to croquet during a visit to his house and I immediately thought it would be a good game to play. I went to Knowles, the main sports shop in Worcester, and bought a croquet set. We had not landscaped the garden so I was able to easily fit in a full size 35 x 28 yards croquet lawn. We also had a tennis court installed and created a paddock for Jill's newly arrived pony – Bambi. Jill and Mark soon learnt to swim and Jill spent so much time with Bambi that Beatrice and I thought we should also take up riding. Beatrice bought a horse and I shared a horse called Sundance with Jeremy's wife, Bridget. I did learn to jump a five bar gate. Having not ridden as a child I never felt in total control and recall one or two frightening moments.

To add to the excitement we bought a red setter puppy. It was a great time. Mark and Jill were growing up and with new interests of riding, swimming, croquet and tennis. We were enjoying our new house and meeting lots of new friends but what we didn't know was that there was a major problem looming.

The following year, 1971, was to see the fulfillment of an idea that had first occurred to me when I wondered why we couldn't heat a house without the paraphernalia of copper cylinders and water tanks in the roof. Why couldn't we heat hot water directly from the mains?

5

The New Idea

There was one big reason why a boiler couldn't take water directly from the mains to provide central heating and hot water. Actually there were 179 reasons: the water companies. In 1970 they were made up of 100 water boards, each comprising two or more local authorities; 50 local authorities and 29 privately owned water companies. They were all regulated by byelaws which did not permit water to be taken straight from the mains supply and directly heated by a boiler. The reason for this was their concern over the possibility of back siphoning of contaminated water. They believed that there must be a physical break in the water supply line.

Could we design a boiler that either satisfied or circumvented the bylaws? If so it had to be the future if we were to be successful since it eliminated so many things: the hot water cylinder, the cold water tanks in the roof space and a considerable amount of pipework. It would be more efficient and cheaper to run, cheaper to install and provide instant unlimited hot water. But first I needed to know how we could get round the water regulations. This was where my old RAF friend Arthur Money, then still working for Yorkshire Imperial Plastics – who just happened to be developing plastic tubing for the water industry – stepped in. He knew the right people in the South Staffordshire Water company to help us. Bernard Hawkin, Anthony Paveley, Bob Wright, who knew the water bylaws backwards, and I, together with Arthur, met up in the Raven Hotel in Droitwich and eventually, after a number of meetings, came up with a design which did not contravene the water bylaws.

We had a dual strategy. First, we needed to patent a prototype combination boiler that would circumvent the bylaws and win the approval of the water companies. Second, we had to work with the government to get the bylaws changed. The water industry was still very fragmented and a major reorganisation was planned, and I knew it was only a matter of time – although quite how much time, I did not then realise. I asked Arthur Money to join us as Technical Sales Manager. He had the job of negotiating with the government departments concerned. The idea was that we would then be in the front seat and ready to take advantage of the changes in the water regulations. Arthur was also to be the project leader of our new boiler – the 'Combi'.

I obtained a joint patent with Bernard Hawkin, Anthony Paveley and Bob Wright. Unfortunately we had to apply for a dispensation for each boiler we sold. This was not helpful but it was a start. The new boiler was to be called 'Heatslave'.

Our prototype Heatslave was oil-fired. It was obvious gas would take over much of the market with the advent of North Sea gas, and we were ready to take advantage of it too, but at that point I could see it made sense to concentrate on oil and become the market leader, albeit a smaller market. Our competitors thought the combination boiler would never happen. They also thought oil would be sidelined into a small market, and of course that was true, but they were also locked into their investment in cast iron production lines – even though natural gas was well on the way, and therefore wouldn't require cast iron to be used.

The decision to convert Britain to natural gas was taken in 1966, and a year later the first North Sea gas was brought ashore at the Easington Terminal in County Durham. It would be ten years before every appliance in the country - about 34 million - was converted from town gas to natural gas, but somehow the perception persisted that boilers would still have to be made of cast iron. Looking back, I can only assume that because the major boiler manufacturers had invested in very comprehensive automated cast iron production lines they did not want to contemplate writing off the investment. It was as if they still believed in something strong and powerful as a material. They thought it would last much longer; that cast iron, not fabricated steel, was the future. Potterton, Glow Worm, Ideal Standard, Thorn, Baxi – they were all producing hundreds of thousands of cast iron boilers. I couldn't compete with their marketing clout and manufacturing capacity. If we were going to succeed we would have to leapfrog them; their lack of interest in the combination boiler and commitment to cast iron would give us the opportunity.

I was confident they were wrong. Our aim was to introduce a light-weight copper heat exchanger, copper being very responsive whereas cast iron is relatively slow to heat up. If the central heating is on, the boiler will be hot and it will provide hot water almost instantaneously when required. But when the central heating is off and the boiler cold, the heat-up time has to be as short as possible. A copper heat exchanger had to be the answer. We had to bide our time and compromise. The market, in my view, was not going to accept a revolution. It had to be evolution, a step by step approach. Firstly we had to convince the wider market, the installers and heating engineers, that the combi boiler was going to work. What we needed was a transitional vehicle that would satisfy British Gas, conservative merchants and heating engineers, yet introduce the new concept. Initially we would use a cast iron boiler. It was a gamble: plumbers could cope with conventional boilers, which were essentially Bunsen burners, but the Heatslave had everything incorporated, including sophisticated electronics. It had many advantages and, being new, there would be a huge learning curve.

One thing installers quickly realised: if you could provide mains pressure hot water, then you could install something that more and more people wanted – a shower. We were a bath-taking nation because we had lousy showers. The head of water was so poor you couldn't get any pressure, but the combi, working directly off the mains, would give you a decent shower, eliminate the airing cupboard with its hot water cylinder, and provide extra space. It became a good selling point. At the same time the boiler itself, being cast iron, was simple technology and British Gas were happy to put it on their approved list, which was important when trying to convince installers about the new concept.

First we had to convince the builders and installers of the merits of mains pressure hot water. I believed it would be too difficult to sell this new concept at the same time as convincing them a fabricated boiler would be durable. We had to start with a cast iron boiler – a very slim one that would prevent the final unit from being too bulky. I found it at Thorn Heating, one of our competitors – initially, buying it from merchants, until we felt we could buy in bigger quantities, when I went directly to Thorn in Newcastle. The chief executive, John Sweet, was himself a Geordie, although he commuted by air from Weybridge every week. He was an interesting guy, a miner's son who had won a scholarship to Cambridge. We built up a good relationship and I found myself driving up to Newcastle regularly. This was before the M42 had been built so it was a long drive but my new Jensen made the journey tolerable.

None of the other British manufacturers, who had almost 100% of the market between them, believed in the combination boiler as a concept. John

Sweet said over dinner one evening: "Cecil, if you're successful, I have to tell you we'll come in and sweep you aside, because we have the marketing strength." "Well," I replied, "we'll have to see about that." They all believed that if we were successful they could move in and push us aside (Thorn disappeared in 1986).

The Heatslave was not an instant success, although it sold well enough, but our traditional oil-fired boilers were continuing to flourish. But I believed in the long sell. Not all our salesmen did, partly because however much time I spent training the team there were always those who preferred to come out with an order for a traditional boiler, whereas the Heatslave tended to be specified first and ordered later. David Jones, who was later to be sales director, believed in the Heatslave. He made a massive breakthrough in Plymouth by convincing the local authority to install gas Heatslaves in their new Estover housing estate, and that opened the door to many people who might have been cautious about the new concept. That was the start of the Heatslave being accepted.

Our oil-fired boilers were going well but we had changed from our old Wallflame burner to the Dynaflame which was technically superior although we ran into massive component unreliability. The early components were handmade and were very good but when they went into volume production they were a disaster. It was devastating to find the electronics were erratic and created many problems, and might have sunk us if we hadn't worked out a massive exchange arrangement with the help of the manufacturer. At one point we were surviving on a wing and a prayer, uncertain as to whether the manufacturer of the electronics would accept any financial responsibility. We had told our suppliers we would claim, but we weren't sure they would pay. Fortunately they did, but they would only compensate us for the costs we incurred solving the problems, not the cost of our reduced sales and the loss of our reputation.

It wasn't an easy thing to deal with, but we decided it had to be turned to some advantage – use the difficulty, as Michael Caine once said. We decided that if one component was faulty we would replace not only that particular one, but all five linked to the problem. Logistically it was quite an operation: we had to get the components to the customer from the manufacturer and get our engineers on the job as swiftly as we could, and we had to employ some sub-contract engineers. I set up half a dozen service centres – the first being in Macclesfield, where my old rugby playing friend Peter Holland's wife Janet said she would take on the task of service administration. Their two daughters were young at the time but Janet was magnificent, operating everything from home. Then we set up similar operations in Exeter, Cambridge, Yorkshire and Scotland. At the same time we built test rigs to test the electronics ourselves, besides going to the manufacturers to check their testing operations. Beatrice's brother Philip was an electronics engineer with the government radar establishment in Malvern, and he was roped in to help us build a testing unit which would reject any component with a problem – every electronics box we sent out was first cycled through the test rig for at least two days. It was a significant operation.

The salesmen heard people say that they would never buy another Worcester boiler. My view was that all of life is a long time: the competition will make mistakes too. You just have to keep knocking on the door. And if the problem can be resolved, and quickly – well, you can claim some success out of the calamity, as we had always found. Customers were heard to say "the engineer came from the factory, he was ever so nice, replaced the boiler and now it works like a charm..." It was a difficult time. We had been let down by the component suppliers but it was clearly our responsibility to overcome the problems and we did.

Despite this major hiccup, the company still made progress during this time. We were even approached by Potterton's, who were the market leaders with about 70% of the gas market. We were gradually overcoming the component problem and we still had faith in the future of the combi so I told them politely that we did not want to sell the company. Potterton pulled out of the oil sector less than five years later. Nevertheless the market was generally buoyant, and there were new competitors: Shell not only decided to make their own boiler but to import a back boiler unit from an Irish company, Waterford Stanley. It was similar to the popular Baxi system with a flame effect fire and a cast iron boiler behind to heat the water. Baxi, a Preston boiler manufacturer, sold hundreds of thousands of their fires. Personally I never believed in the concept – if you were going to have a flame effect fire, then have one, but the last place to put the boiler, in my view, was behind it.

Shell decided to start manufacturing their own boilers in Birmingham however, adding the name Harcal to the market. They promised it would be quieter than anybody else's and it was, because it was so highly insulated. It was larger and also much heavier and more expensive to manufacture. It seems odd to me that an oil company should tie themselves to one manufacturer, particularly as they would have to subsidise each boiler, which was expensive to produce. We, in the mean time, had developed a much smaller and equally quiet boiler. It was also much cheaper to produce so it was not surprising that after only two years Shell stopped production of the Harcal. I discovered that Shell had also ceased to import the back boilers from Waterford in order to manufacture them in Birmingham. I thought there might be a short term opportunity there because Shell had heavily marketed the Waterford name and established a significant demand for the product.

I flew to Dublin, took the train to Waterford and concluded a deal on the back boilers, which would now be called Firefly Waterford. The sales director kindly offered to drive me back to Dublin to catch a train to Belfast – at that time there were no flights to Northern Ireland because of the Troubles. As it had the casting facility, Waterford Stanley had diversified into cast iron cookware at the time, and a very long and winding drive back to Dublin was made even longer by my companion's tale of a dissatisfied customer who had arrived at their stand at the Dublin Show to insist that his frying pan had exploded in the middle of the night and had the bits in a paper bag to prove it. My driver occasionally interrupted his story, particularly as we became embedded in the mayhem that was Dublin traffic, by assuring me that we would be all right, that he'd get me to the station. Eventually he changed his reassurance to: "Well, now, you see that building in the distance... if you get out now and run like hell, you might catch the train". I had a case full of extremely heavy samples and I hadn't got a ticket, but I did make the train, and just as it drew out I saw the cheerful sales director beaming through the window: "I told you you'd make it, I told you you'd make it!" I was exhausted; it took about an hour for me to recover.

We sold these back boiler fires by the container load, and because they went directly from Ireland to the merchants we not only made a decent margin on each one but established a relationship with some distributors we hadn't previously been able to break into. But I still didn't believe in them, and by the summer of 1972 sales had dropped. Waterford Stanley then came to me and said they'd ceased production but had around 3,000 in stock; would I take them with an extra discount of £50 each? £150,000 was a lot of money, it was tempting, but I said no – and thank God I did because if I had that might well have sunk us in 1973. I think people liked the flame effect out of sentiment, because the country had only relatively recently changed from coal fires to central heating. People still like looking at a fire.

In 1971 Edward Heath's Conservative government began formal negotiations to join the European Economic Community - too late, I believe. When

I first went to France at the end of the 1960s I learned a lot about the way things worked. Distributors in Europe didn't particularly want a new boiler. In fact, I believe European manufacturers had a strategy to keep Britain out of their markets while they got themselves organised. They set up technical barriers designed to make them very difficult for outsiders to overcome. There were no independent test houses or standards, so if a British manufacturer wanted to sell its products in France or Germany it had to submit them to the French or German test houses. European standards were a long way off at the time. I was told that as Britain was not in the EEC our products were always at the bottom of the list and there were many delays because of misinterpretation of the technical standards. Whilst this was going on, the French and German manufacturing companies were merging and consolidating and so becoming much stronger. The distribution outlets were also developing relationships with these companies. This combination of factors made it very difficult for British manufacturers to establish outlets for their products in France and Germany.

Nevertheless we went back to Paris in 1971 and took a working boiler with us, because one of the things we had developed and which they had not was a quiet boiler. We received a good deal of interest in France and decided we needed someone to get things off the ground, so I advertised in the *Daily Telegraph* for a 'Mr Europe'. That was how we found Charles Fenner, Swiss born, speaking French and German and living in England. We followed up three or four enquiries in France together, got on well, and he became Our Man in Europe. We began to sell quite a significant number of boilers into France through a very energetic entrepreneur who set up in Lille as our agent for Northern France.

In those days the Board of Trade assisted companies to exhibit abroad, paying for the delivery of equipment (although only going out, not coming back). If English was not the spoken language, the translation costs were paid for. We had taken advantage of the scheme in Paris in 1969, in Frankfurt in 1970 and having learnt from the experience, went back to Paris in 1971 where we were successful. That same year the Board of Trade supported a Building Exhibition held at the Sydney Cricket Ground in Australia. A Japanese company had visited us in Worcester and talked to us about building our products for the Japanese market. So our next attempt to export involved a trip to Japan. This was to further our talks, exhibit our products in Australia and come back via South Africa where we had already established a successful agency. The Board of Trade also conducted surveys for companies to find out whether a country might provide a potential market for their products.

I travelled economy class and the flight to Tokyo in 1970 took about 17 hours. I was tired when I got off the plane, to be met by Mr Komato who had visited Worcester. The drive into Tokyo entailed frequent sudden accelerations followed by screeching of brakes as we shot into vacated slots in the congested traffic. It seemed this was one way of relieving the boredom of a long slow drive into the city centre. I had hoped to be taken to my hotel, but instead I was taken to the old Japanese building which housed one of the city's major domestic appliance companies. All the doorways were about five foot six so that I had to duck many times before I arrived at the meeting room. The entire board was waiting to greet me: about ten board members and the chief executive. The protocol was that they were introduced in order of seniority, the Chief Executive being the last person to enter the room. I bowed to all of them, and they bowed to me, after which they said they would like to ask me a few questions. It was a surreal experience. We sat down in a circle and I kept almost falling asleep, but they kept asking questions and then laughing and chattering among themselves. I was becoming faintly paranoid. What were they laughing at? There was no explanation. It would then go quiet and the spokesman would say, "I have another question for you Mr Duckworth". Occasionally they would glance at me and then would go into long conversations. After a 17 hour flight and an 11 hour time change I was having difficulty in staying awake. So to keep awake I looked around and imagined I was a prisoner of war and they were interrogating me and I didn't know the answers. I remember being deep in thought about how I was going to get out of this dilemma alive but eventually I was taken by car to a super hotel that would compete with any five star western hotel. On arrival I booked in and my Japanese escort said to me, "We have two more questions for you". At the time I was like a zombie and insisted I had to go to bed. He then told me the board had arranged dinner for me at 8.00pm which was in four hours time. I thought after four hours sleep I might just make it so I agreed and as we parted said, "I'll see you at eight". I got to my room, hit the pillow and went out like a light. The next thing I was aware of was the telephone ringing. Coming to from a deep sleep I answered the phone. "Mr Komato here, it's eight pm. I'm in the lobby". After a long hot shower I eventually got out of the lift feeling half alive and heard the now familiar words, "Mr Duckworth we have another question for you". I finally said this must be the last question and eventually we left the hotel.

I was then introduced to Japanese food. I know it is very popular today, but I wasn't accustomed to it then. Japanese men enjoy going out on their expense accounts, but I was intrigued to find that Japanese ladies would also go out dressed in kimonos, meeting their friends in perfectly respectable bars where they could have a drink or take tea. Often they were alone, or in pairs, and were happy to talk to those men who spoke to them. There was no sign of flirtation: at about ten o'clock they all departed to go home.

However I had to concentrate on dinner. "Do you like asparagus, Mr Duckworth?" I said yes, I love asparagus, I come from the centre of asparagus growing in England. But this was something different. It was a single spear of asparagus, about half an inch thick, quite raw and served on a bed of ice. I persevered, but it was extraordinarily tough. However I got through it eventually, trying not to remember English asparagus, steamed and dripping with butter. Then, having finished, they insisted I had another one – quite an ordeal.

We had lots of meetings. I had been told that the Japanese are very thorough and will address every issue in great detail before making the decision to go ahead. The company we were talking to was one of the largest domestic appliance manufacturers in Japan. The board had made a decision to enter the central heating market. They realised that Europe was well developed in this area so instead of starting from scratch they came to an agreement to build appliances under licence. They had gone around the major exhibitions of Europe and had chosen our oil-fired boiler range and Heatslave hot water unit. They had visited our factory and we had supplied samples so they knew a lot about our company and our products before my visit. We had many more meetings, dining out every night, a great evening at a geisha house, and after five days they said they would go ahead. However, protocol being what it was, their Chief Executive would come to England and sign the agreement. Initially we would receive £5,000 as a part payment and then receive a royalty payment for each product they produced. I left for Australia in a happy frame of mind for two reasons: firstly, our trip was more than paid for and secondly, we would have the royalties coming in over the years ahead. Ken Hamilton joined me in Sydney.

Australia was a hard sell, particularly in Sydney where air conditioning combined with heating is important, their summers being much hotter than ours. The simplest way to achieve this is to have a unit that can be switched from heating to cooling, rather than the water fed radiator systems we have. We found some interest in Melbourne, which was much cooler, with a climate similar to England, but it wasn't going to be a big market for us. We did sell the exhibition boilers and establish a small outlet which worked for a number of years.

We then moved to South Africa where we had a distributor. There was a feeling that as television was on its way there, people would be more likely to stay indoors and would therefore need central heating. We made some progress, and insurance against a downturn in the UK - besides, I felt we had a responsibility to export overseas.

Travel had given me a new perspective, too. I realised how we had been left behind by going so late into the Common Market, as it was then. Britain had led the industrial revolution and we had the Empire to feed into, but as local markets developed so those old ties had eroded. The big home market became Europe. Manufacturing had been a low priority for all the political parties in this country. Secretaries of State for Industry changed frequently and didn't have time to understand or grasp what support is required. I still hear MPs say it doesn't matter who owns a company because we are not only European but we live in a global economy; the self-interested people in the City of London, the merchant bankers, the accountants and the lawyers, say it doesn't matter, because they only care about their bonuses. But when looking at our present borrowing and the massive gap in our balance of payments, I think we have to come to the conclusion that we have got it wrong. In my view the Secretary of State for Industry should be equal second in the Cabinet with the Chancellor and the Home Secretary. One of government's priorities has to be wealth creation. If the country is wealthy everything else becomes so much easier. In my view it would be a good idea to look how the Germans run their industry. We now have a Prime Minister and a Chancellor backing industry - I hope we are not too late!!

On the other hand, it is possible to get through a disaster and make a new start. As I was about to discover.

6

Oil Crisis

I had always had some concern about the vulnerability of oil. The Heatslave was not a standard gas fired boiler and although I felt it was the future, our golden egg at the time was oil – but the company was 90% dependent on oil. There had been a problem in 1967 when the Israelis attacked Egypt in the Six Day War, but it had been over so quickly that nothing changed. Now there was a new player in the game, increasingly aware of its power: the Organisation of Petroleum Exporting Companies (OPEC). In 1973 OPEC, which included the Arab oil exporting countries plus Egypt, Syria and Tunisia, produced over 50% of the world's crude oil. I read the newspapers with some care as I watched its increasing confidence. And on October 6, 1973, Yom Kippur, the holiest day in the Jewish calendar, Egypt and Syria attacked Israel.

At first, as I watched every news bulletin, I was reassured by those who said that OPEC would not cause a problem for the West because until then the relationship between them had been reasonably stable, and in any case OPEC was not due to meet for several months. But I became increasingly apprehensive. I could see that if the war continued for much longer, we would have a problem. Sure enough, despite Egypt's initial success and the Syrian gains in the Golan Heights, the Israelis launched a counter-offensive and finally advanced into Egypt itself. It was a humiliating reversal. On October 17 the Arab members of OPEC declared they would impose an oil embargo on the United States, Britain and France and increased prices by 400%. A week later the United Nations managed to broker a ceasefire to end the war – but the price of oil went from three dollars a barrel to twelve.

It was like the Suez crisis all over again. There was talk of petrol rationing; ration coupons were printed, although in the end never used. People were terrified of investing in oil central heating. Virtually overnight we lost 90% of our business. During October and November we did not receive a single order. We were left with the Heatslave making up about 10% of the business.

I called the sales team in. We had about 17 salesmen at the time. I had to be straight with them. I said: "Look, I don't want to fire you, but I can only keep three people. The rest of you can always come back, but in the meantime you must find another job". There wasn't any animosity because they all understood the situation. At the time they could easily get another job: the UK economy was actually overheated because Anthony Barber, Chancellor of the Exchequer in Edward Heath's Tory government, had gone for growth. Companies not affected by the price of oil had a full order book.

I went back to Morgan Crucible and although they had a new supplier by then, we started making some furnaces for them and took on making various pieces of equipment that I don't think anyone else wanted to make. We were exceptionally good at welding and making metal components and electrical assemblies, and we were very good at making boilers but did not have the skills to make other products. To get these skills would take time which was something we didn't have. But I managed to keep one or two very good practical engineers which was very necessary in finding new work to keep the company going.

Our house was also on the line to the bank. I never mentioned this to Beatrice. I didn't want to worry her. The curious thing is that in the depths of the crisis I always felt there would be a way out of the morass. Perhaps I was clinging to such straws as the fact that we owned our own factory outright, and we'd had some fat in our bank balance. But I could have lost everything. And that's what you have to do in business. The bank was looking for security, so I had to risk everything we owned, basically. People tend to forget that. And it might have happened... if it hadn't been for a piece of blotting paper, but more about this later. Obviously I considered different routes to follow, but as to 'what might happen if...' well, I didn't really think about that. Perhaps I didn't let myself. I suspect there is an element of will involved. If you spend all your time worrying about the catastrophe, you probably don't concentrate on the solution.

You could argue that we had put too many eggs in one basket with regard to our oil-fired boilers, and with hindsight you might say it was a risky thing to do – and of course it was; but in the early days of developing a business you are vulnerable. If you try to do lots of things to ensure you are less vulnerable, you would probably not do any of them very well, so then what's the chance of being successful? It's frustrating in the early stages of developing a company because you know what you want to do, but you do not have the finance or the volume of business to develop a management team, it's a Catch 22 situation. At this time the only solution was for me to work eight days a week.

Ultimately, in my case, we simply had to produce a product that householders were happy with and would recommend to their friends; that the installer liked and felt would make his business secure, and would provide the merchant with margins he's pleased with. This takes time. Then there are all the other commercial issues that you have to be good at, just to do business, delivering on time, invoicing, after sales service, technical support – and the ability to put things right if they go wrong.

We had to accept that it was an international crisis that nobody had predicted. The timing of these events is often a matter of luck. If it had happened three or four years later we would have been able to ride the storm; three or four years earlier we would have had no chance. When it happened we did have a number of things going for us. One, we had our own factory which was paid for so there was no rent to pay; two, we had been successful so we had money in the bank and three, the British economy was booming so those people we no longer required could find other employment.

The two years following the 1973 oil crisis were bleak. Our oil-fired range of boilers was selling well prior to October but because there was now uncertainty of the supply of oil and a quadrupling of the price, there was no market. The price of oil before 17 October 1973 was cheaper than gas but that was no longer the case. The choice was now simple: if you lived in a gas area you would have a gas boiler installed. If you lived outside the gas area the choice was solid fuel, LPG or oil.

Solid fuel had limited appeal and LPG was even more expensive than oil. So we knew oil would come back in the rural areas. The question was, when? Could we hang on? Most of the small manufacturers disappeared and Potterton, who had been the largest manufacturer when I started in 1962, discontinued their range of oil-fired boilers. Unfortunately there were a lot of boilers in stock at the merchants and those manufacturers who pulled out of oil sold their stock off at below cost prices. We lost 90% of our sales. For almost twelve months we were only able to sell a handful of boilers. Sales of our gas-fired Heatslave Combi did increase but it was difficult because of having to get dispensation from the water boards for each sale.

I also had another major problem. My old friend and colleague Ken Hamilton had developed what appeared to be a Walter Mitty approach to life, so that monthly accounts weren't appearing on time, if at all, at a time when both the bank and I needed to know exactly what our financial situation was on a daily basis. Ken had developed a real drink problem, which I hadn't fully realised at the time.

Looking back, it had begun when we left the discipline of the ladies at the Locomotive pub. I didn't know anything about alcoholism, but I do recall when we went for a drink occasionally at the Ketch in Kempsey there was a little ledge under the counter, and if Ken bought a round of drinks he would buy three for himself and line them up on the ledge. I wasn't aware how far down that road he was, but the oil crisis was a tipping point for him. The whole world seemed to be tumbling down in his life. I tried to talk to him about it and he agreed he would cut down on his drinking and produce the accounts on time, particularly as my friendly bank manager, Vic Carter, had also heard about his problem by now.

One of the bank's employees went to the same pub as Ken and reported back to Vic. As a result, Vic asked me: "Has Ken got a drink problem?" I naturally played down the problem but Vic told me that the regional Head Office wanted monthly figures from us. I told Ken, who always apologised for letting me down, that in future the figures must be produced on time.

I suppose we had four or five serious meetings over this period. He would agree not to drink during the day, and I proposed he limit his evening drinking to three pints. Looking back I now realise he had already got a problem that he could not control. Finally I told him that I couldn't go on like this. He was simply driving me crackers. I discovered too late that he would come in to work in the morning, make it obvious that he was around if I was there, and then say he was going to the bank. He would go out at eleven and would always come back just before one o'clock, so I wasn't aware of the length of time he was away from his office. Then he would leave just after one o'clock and come back at two, again making sure I was aware of him being around. I wasn't suspicious; far from checking up on him, I had thought he had given up drinking during the day. Then I discovered he had simply stopped drinking in the Ketch, a pub which I passed on my way home for lunch. What I hadn't realised was that he had started to go to a pub which was in the centre of the village of Kempsey where we both lived. The difference was I didn't pass this pub on my way home.

We had what I thought was a final showdown. I told Ken that he either gave up drinking during the day – what he did at night was his problem – or he had to go. I had to have the monthly accounts on time, I had to present them to the bank and in any case I needed them. We had a whole new set of circumstances to deal with and if he couldn't give up drinking and deal with the company's finances, then I would buy his shares at a nominal price. We shook hands on it. We had had lots of agreements which were not honoured. I remember saying: "I mean it, Ken. This is the very last time."

Things were fine for a few days. I did check a couple of times to see if he was in one of the pubs. Then one day I drove off the M5, on my way back to Worcester. I'd been up since six that morning. And I saw his car driving into the car park of the Swan Inn, a pub I would not normally pass. I was absolutely furious. I decided I would confront him in the pub, but I parked beside his car, and for some reason he had left the car door unlocked. I don't know why I checked the door, but I did. I thought no, I'm not going to go into the pub. Perhaps I couldn't face it. I got a piece of paper out of my car and wrote on it: "Thanks for letting me down". And I left it in his car and closed the door.

I had always taken the view that Ken and I had started Worcester Engineering together, and we'd finish it together. We had been friends for years. But alcoholism is an insidious disease. The day after that final encounter in the car park of the Swan, Ken disappeared on a complete bender. His family was worried – his wife of course, like Ken himself, was a close friend. They had a young son, Paul. And Ken's father came to see me, asking where he was, so I had to go through the whole history with him. He wanted me to give Ken another chance. I told him I couldn't. The situation had gone past the point of no return. He said he was very disappointed in me: "I'm sure in your heart you want to help him, you've been such great friends." "You don't realise," I told him, "I just can't do it anymore. It's exhausting me. I'm trying to keep the company going, trying to manage this brinkmanship as to whether we can survive or not, and Ken isn't helping at all, in fact the reverse. He's destroyed our friendship. I can't help him, I don't know anything about alcoholism. All I can say is that he has a massive problem, and I can't live with it."

I was then working late most evenings and at weekends. One afternoon I had a call from my three musketeer friends who had helped design the Heatslave and were involved with the water industry: Anthony Paveley, Bob Wright and Bernard Hawkin. We arranged a meeting at the factory at six o'clock that evening. My car was in for a service so it wasn't parked in its usual place. During the afternoon Bob rang to say they were running late. I said, "Don't worry, I'll be here."

I was in my office when I suddenly saw a car appear outside. It was Ken's car. In it was not only him but his father, his wife Liz and young son Paul who must have been about five or six years old. I didn't move. I could only think: "Oh God, do I want a confrontation with the whole family?" I still didn't move. Then I heard them in Ken's office, which was next to mine. Their voices were raised and they were arguing among themselves. I could hear Liz saying, "Well, I told you to organise a meeting with Cecil, and you haven't. He's obviously not here, his car's not here." And his father said: "No wonder he wants to get rid of you, you can't even organise a meeting with him."

I still didn't move or make a sound. Then, abruptly, my telephone rang. The light indicated the call was from Ken's office next door. I just sat still and thought: "Shall I answer it?" And my next thought was: "No". So I still didn't move. Suddenly I heard Liz say, "Paul, stop playing with that machine!" And then I realised the little boy was simply pushing the switches down and he'd pushed down the one marked 'CD'. I heard Ken's father say: "Come on, then. He's not here. We've made a mess of it again. We'll have to arrange a proper meeting; bring all your books, take everything, all the books from your office..."   I heard them leave; they went down the corridor towards reception – just as my three friends arrived.

I could hear the conversation. They explained they were here to see me, that they had arranged a meeting. "Well, he's not here," Ken's father said. But Bob Wright said, "That's strange, I only telephoned him an hour ago".

I didn't want to miss them. I hadn't got a car to chase after them And knew they were about to go. I thought: I will have to move. I opened my office door and stepped out into the corridor. I will remember that moment for the rest of my life. Ken was locking his office door, next to mine. He had a bunch of ledgers under his arm and his pipe hanging from his mouth. As I appeared, he looked at me as though I was a ghost. In that moment he realised I had been there all along, that I heard everything. I said: "Hi, Ken." He could hardly speak: "Oh... I didn't – I didn't think – I didn't think you were here." His face was white. I just looked past him and spoke to Anthony Paveley: "Hello, Tony, come on in..."

Neither Ken nor his family ever contacted me again. He went on another bender, disappearing for several days. I hadn't wanted to engender that desperation, and this time I knew I wasn't responsible for it. I wrote to him to say how I was sorry things had turned out the way they had, and I hoped he would understand why I couldn't go on. I expected him to honour our agreement that I would buy him out. The sum involved was £15,000, which was 50% of the nominal value of the company. It doesn't sound much now but then in 1975, when we were in such trouble, it was a lot of money.

And we were in trouble. While all that was going on I was having problems with cash flow. Some weeks I had difficulty in meeting the wage bill. Vic Carter, my bank manager, was being as helpful as he could, but he was now under scrutiny from the man above him and said we couldn't exceed our overdraft. It was simply no longer possible. Stories of people promising 'the cheque's in the post' are legion, but the reality was that it was exactly like that: I just didn't know if a cheque would arrive in time to pay the wages. I had to say to Vic that I couldn't manage it, but I would be able to get a cheque to him by Tuesday or Wednesday. On four separate occasions, when a cheque came in for payment which would have taken me over the balance, Vic said, "Well... I'll have to slip it behind the blotting paper." I survived... for the sake of a piece of blotting paper. And I didn't let him down: I always did get the cheque that was in the post, if not by the Tuesday, then Wednesday. Vic, of course, did not know for certain that I would be able to cover the outstanding balance. It was great that he should believe in me to that extent and incredible that he would take the chance.

The financial information was not up-to-date and neither I nor the bank had had monthly trading accounts for over two months. I rang Roger Smith, the senior partner at Rabjohns, our accountants, to see if they could loan me someone capable of getting us up to date and provide the bank with accurate information. Vic Carter at the bank was always helpful and had become a great friend. It was difficult, because our friendship had been built on mutual trust. I was now in danger of destroying that trust, particularly as Vic now had his regional manager breathing down his neck. It was a massive dilemma at the time.

Fortunately Rabjohns had recently taken on a senior accountant by the name of Nigel Collis, with the intention of him becoming a partner. He had not established a client base and was immediately available. Nigel quickly got a grip of the situation. We had many problems at the time. Inflation was rising rapidly so all our bought out items were costing more, whereas previously they had been going down in price due to increased sales. With our sales going up this meant we could order in larger quantities and so qualify for improved terms. We had been flying blind so it was a massive relief to have up-to-date financial information and, at the same time, be able to keep the bank happy.

After Nigel had been with us for about six months I had established that he would make an excellent Financial Director. Nigel was enthusiastic and became part of the team with Roger Tomlinson, Arthur Money and myself. I also agreed to give them 5% each of the equity, assuming I could conclude my agreement with Ken Hamilton.

Sales were gradually improving. We were selling more Heatslaves, so production was expanding, and we began to sell the occasional oil-fired boiler as well. We lost a lot of money in 1974 – about £62,000 – but I believed that because we owned our own factory, inflation meant its value had probably risen by a similar amount so on paper at least we were not too badly affected. It was the cash flow that was the problem. We didn't need the blotting paper any more, which was just as well because Vic Carter was suddenly rushed into hospital for a major bowel operation and a new sub-manager replaced him. Not only was he not easy to talk to, I couldn't get to him in the first place; he didn't want to talk to me, or so it appeared. He also wanted to reduce our overdraft. I pointed out that we had been caught by an international oil crisis which no one had predicted – and I was sure he hadn't. I told him trading was slowly improving, so why wouldn't he support me?

I began to talk to various people about a capital injection into the company. If Ken honoured our agreement and I could raise the £15,000, I would then own the whole company outright, so I could sell off say 20% or 25% of the equity to a third party. I talked to one or two merchant banks to see if they would take some of the equity, but it was very difficult to put a value on the business because we were still in an uncertain situation. It was also difficult to paint a picture that showed the future was going to be rosy. For one thing, in rural areas where there had been no real alternative to oil there was now the opportunity to have mains gas. The government had carried out a massive programme of expanding the gas mains into rural areas of the country in the build up to the privatisation of British Gas, so a lot of people were now able to replace their oil boiler with gas. It was inevitable that the oil-fired market would be much smaller. How many oil-fired boiler manufacturers would survive? As it happened, fortunately for us, most of them didn't – we were the only independent private manufacturer left. To an outsider, we did not look like an attractive investment at the time. If we were to get a cash injection, it would have to be an act of faith.

I then went to see Peter Walker, by then a very good friend. He was no longer in government, the Conservatives having lost the election in February 1974.

I told Peter that oil-fired boilers were coming back, and we had this great new idea of the combination boiler which I was sure was going to take off. In the short term our priority had to be selling our oil-fired range of boilers. To achieve this, I would need to promote and advertise our product range so that the installers and builders' merchants would have confidence we would survive. I would also need to take on additional salesmen. That was one of the reasons we required additional funds, the other being the promotion and further developing of our Heatslave Combi. After the deal with Ken I would own 100% of the shares so I could easily sell off 25% of the equity. Peter then took me by total surprise when he said, "Look Cecil, this crisis wasn't of your making, you've got a very good product which has been very successful and I think you have huge potential with your combi boiler. Why don't I and a few of my friends get together and see if we can put some money in?" I was naturally over the moon with Peter's proposal and said I would need to work out how much money I required but having done some preliminary work it would not be less than £100,000. His immediate response was, "You always need a little more than you first think. Why don't we inject £125,000 for 25% of the equity?" It was quite incredible. I had only gone to Peter's house to discuss my problems and one hour later I had the solution. Within a week Peter rang me to say they could raise the money. He told me that Tim Yeo, who later became a fellow MP, had been investing some money for him and he and a few other friends would be the investors. It was also agreed that Tim became a director and he proved to be a great asset.

There was one small anxiety at the back of my mind. I still hadn't got a piece of paper from Ken Hamilton: the share certificate. We had agreed on £15,000, but Ken had always stayed in Worcester Engineering because he thought 'if Cecil thinks there's a future in it, I'm staying in there'. If he now discovered I had found a wealthy backer to inject some cash he might just change his mind... and that could blow the whole thing out of the water. But Ken was true to his word and sold his shares to me.

I saw Ken only a couple of times after that, and then by chance. His marriage split up and I suppose we had nothing left to say to one another. I heard that he had managed to beat the alcoholism – indeed, he became local president of Alcoholics Anonymous. Sometime after that, someone I knew slightly came over and asked if he might have a word with me. He was the landlord of the Cricketer pub in Angel Place in the centre of Worcester. "Did you know," he said, "that your old colleague Ken has lunch in my pub every day?"

"I didn't think he drank anymore," I replied.

"He doesn't. He drinks orange juice. And I didn't come to tell you that, but I know he would love to see you. You could call in and see him one day, perhaps?"

I thanked him, and said I would. And once or twice I thought, well, I'll just drop in to the Cricketer and see Ken. But somehow there are never enough hours in the day, life was so busy. So I didn't. And then he died. He had a sudden heart attack and someone simply heard a thud on the floor. I will always regret not seeing him. Perhaps I should have done it anyway, without being prompted. Ken and I had some great times together. He was fun. And when he was sober he was a very good accountant. I would have liked to have talked everything through with him. Perhaps I should have realised earlier how far down the road of alcoholism he had gone, but I didn't really understand it then. We were both young together. I still feel sad when I think of him.

7

Playing Poker

It would have been sensible to sell the Jensen. It cost about a thousand pounds a service and it needed one every three months or so. It was still worth quite a bit of money. But if I did sell it - what kind of signal would that send out to our employees and customers? Instead I decided to have it re-sprayed and change the number plate. It would look like new. I couldn't afford CD 1, at least I didn't think so, if it existed, but I looked through the numbers in the *Sunday Times* and found CD 6700. I used a little creative accounting to suggest that the 6700 indicated the number of boilers we were making... And to all intents and purposes I had a new Jensen. I did have one slight anxiety however: to cut the servicing costs, I had gone to a local garage which was much cheaper but not very good so as a result the Jensen didn't always start. Distributors, merchants, all sorts of people tended to come out and wave me goodbye in the car park after a visit, but I was always concerned that it might fail to start on a vital occasion. Although I could put the bonnet up and fix the problem, it would rather destroy the image.

Jensen had an extraordinary range of colours. My Interceptor was Aztec Gold. You certainly couldn't miss it in a car park... which had its uses.

By 1975 the fight back had begun, but we were by no means out of the wood. I had to search for any opportunity to keep us afloat, despite the fact that things were picking up. At the time I was regularly driving up to Gateshead to visit Thorn Heating in connection with their production of the cast iron gas boiler for our Heatslave. It was a four hour journey then and I would usually stay over at the Gosford Park Hotel with the managing director, John Sweet, who appreciated their excellent wine cellar.

It was on one of these visits, when walking round the Thorn works with John, that I noticed all his oil-fired boilers stacked on the shelves, as yet unsold. Nevertheless the mood in the country was already changing. Oil was once more becoming a sensible choice for central heating in the rural areas when it was realised they could get supplies and the alternative to oil was not very appealing. The market had begun to turn. Thorn were beginning to sell their oil boilers again. They had to make the decision as to whether to get out of oil altogether or to stay in and continue manufacturing.

I said, "You're not really geared up for manufacturing those boilers, are you, now you've reorganized the works to concentrate on gas? I'm buying your cast iron gas boilers, why don't you reciprocate and let me make your oil-fired boilers for you? I've got the capacity. I'll make them much better, too, because with all due respect the one you currently have on those shelves isn't as good as mine." Which was true: for one thing Worcester Engineering had now incorporated the much quieter pressure jet burner, but Thorn had not. Also oil-fired boilers were our business. We had cut back so we could survive but we had kept our development department going and as a result we had a better product than Thorn.

John Sweet thought about this, and on a subsequent visit said: "We've discussed your proposal. If the price is right, we will get you to manufacture our units." I went away with the drawings, came up with a price and went back; they accepted and gave me quite a significant order. It would take us forward twelve months with an option for a further year. For us it meant a way of using the spare capacity we still had as a result of the oil crisis.

I knew the demand for oil would never go back to what it once was. People on the edge of cities, in the suburbs, were now within reach of the gas main. It eroded the potential for the future to the point where I believed it would halve the market. Many of the larger boiler manufacturers felt it wasn't worth continuing with domestic oil-fired boilers. But if we could be a major player in a smaller market – well, we could survive. In the end we were the only private company who did.

So when John Sweet said they would give me the order, I knew the tide had turned.

Then he said, "I'll just have a word..." His directors were not quite as sure: he joined them in the next room for a discussion. I could hear a little of what was said, including the sales director's cautious comment: "Look, John, we're giving Cecil this very large order. Are you sure he's financially OK?"

I thought, oh God... this is not what I want to hear. But it was a perfectly reasonable question of course. Then I heard John's reply: "Cecil? Financially

OK? For God's sake, have you seen his car out there in the car park?" The sales director replied: "Well, I thought I'd just mention it."

John said firmly "There's no question about Cecil's financial standing."

I breathed a sigh of relief to myself. "Yes...!"

As I left I suspected they were all watching from the office window. I could see the Jensen – it was even more mustard coloured after the re-spray than before. As I approached it I thought: Now, you will start, won't you? It did.

We manufactured Thorn's oil-fired boilers for several years, and we bought more and more of their cast iron boilers. The combi boiler was starting to become profitable. Life mid-1975 was looking up. And we were not the only people looking at combination boilers. A news item in the *Financial Times* intrigued me. A company called Delta Appliances had introduced a version of a combination unit called Delglo, although it was not as advanced as ours and did not produce hot water at mains pressure. Delglo was owned by the Delta Metal Company, whose chairman was seeking to sell all loss-making companies in the group before the annual general meeting – which, as it happened, was only two months away. Boilers were currently being manufactured at two of its sites, one in Blackpool and one in Clay Cross, a former mining town in Derbyshire.

I found out that the chairman of the division, a Mr Dalgleish, was based in Droitwich. I wrote to him to explain that I understood the Delglo manufacturing operation was to be sold and that we would be very interested. What I didn't know then was that one of our major competitors, Trianco, had just pulled out of prolonged and painful negotiations to buy the company. My letter arrived on Mr Dalgleish's desk at a timely moment. When I didn't get an immediate answer I rang him up and asked him if I was right to think they wanted to sell – and if so, could I talk to him? He said, "Well, I'm listening to what you say, it may be worthwhile to meet. When were you thinking of?" "Well, you're only in Droitwich – say, about 30 minutes?" "That's refreshing," he said, startled. "Right, I'll see you in half an hour."

Mr Dalgliesh was guarded. This was before Margaret Thatcher's reforms in industrial relations: the unions were still protecting jobs, and there was concern that closing Delglo would lead to repercussions at other factories in the Delta group. Indeed, he gave me the clear indication that I was wasting his time. He asked what my plans were, pointing out that time was important, so I told him I would let him know in three days' time. Once again, a little taken aback, he said my approach was remarkably refreshing.

It looked to me as though the Delglo operation was worth about £700,000 as a going concern, but it was not in a thriving area and there were redundancy costs to consider, and the potential reaction from the unions. If the factory was sold off with the machinery, the knockdown price would probably be no more than £300,000. I wrote to Mr Dalgliesh and offered him £350,000 - half its value as a going concern. Of course I hadn't got £350,000. I would have to sell the idea to the bank.

I was still with NatWest, where the previous bank manager, Vic Carter, had been so helpful with the blotting paper. But the new manager was unable to make decisions. Frustrated by his attitude, I said I wanted to talk to the person who was able to make decisions: he said the new structure didn't allow that. I explained that I was not happy with that and I would like to meet the regional manager, with whom I had had previous problems – which I did, only to be met with the line that all decisions were taken at regional level, but I could always talk to the branch manager. That circular argument led me back to Ted Farrell at Barclays. Ted was the bank manager who had refused to lend me the money for the extension to the Diglis factory – which was why we had then changed to Vic Carter at NatWest. Perhaps he had observed our success with a chastened eye. This time, I said I needed an urgent response, it had to be dealt with *now* – was he interested? He said he'd be round in half an hour.

In fact he decided to bring along his industrial expert as well. I outlined the opportunity to buy Delglo, that it would assure us a magnificent opportunity to recover and get us back to the pre-1973 situation. Yes, there were some unknowns, the Delgo gas-fired boiler for instance was currently made in Blackpool and we would move it to Clay Cross. I knew all about oil-fired boilers but nothing about Delglo. However we sat down and went through the figures.

"So you want to borrow £350,000 from us?" Ted said at last. "And what are you going to put in?" I said I was putting in £350,000.

Ted looked at me and said, "I don't understand."

"Because I'm buying the company for £350,000 less than it's worth."

Ted replied, "They'll love that at head office."

"Well," I said. "That's the reality. Nobody else could buy the company at half price, so that's my contribution."

Ted Farrell went away to 'think about that'... and in the meantime Mr Dalgliesh rang me and said: "I've got your letter. My first reaction is that you can go and jump in the River Severn. But there are jobs involved. So maybe it's worth meeting up. When can you come over?" I said half an hour. Even then, when we began to talk about me buying Delglo, I again got the distinct impression that he felt I hadn't got the money. He eventually agreed to accept my offer, providing the deal could be concluded before Delta's AGM, which was now only ten days away. I had no idea whether I could.

"Yes," I said, "I can meet the deadline."

Now I had agreed a deal, I figured out it would help my negotiations with the bank. The following day I went back to Barclays and said I'd got a deal, provided they backed me. Ted said, "Yes, we'll back you – but we'd like you to raise a mortgage on the Clay Cross factory. You said it was worth about £200,000?" Barclays said they would lend us £150,000 but were still concerned about our working capital.

We were operating 'just in time' (JIT) which became very fashionable a few years later. I now find it very interesting because we had been doing so from day one. It meant we didn't need working capital because we bought in all materials and components and didn't pay for them until the end of the month following the month of delivery, by which time we had turned them into a boiler and would have received payment. The concept that working capital was not a necessary requirement was one that Ted and his colleagues didn't fully appreciate, but they accepted it – as long as I found £200,000 by mortgaging the factory.

Obviously Barclays had cold feet about lending us the full £350,000. I rang Peter Walker, who put me in touch with two or three people in the City who might be willing to help us with a mortgage, but as soon as the name Clay Cross was mentioned they just didn't want to know. What had been a mining village in Derbyshire had become identified with eleven councillors on Clay Cross district council who in 1972 refused to increase council rents, a stance which led them to be surcharged, banned from public office for five years and, eventually, made bankrupt. On the Thursday before the Delta

AGM, I was in London and had to conclude the financial position by the following Monday - the day we were to hand over the cheque and complete the deal. The problem was I could not find anyone to provide a mortgage on the Clay Cross factory. I had spent three days going from one financial house to another, finding no interest until I came across the Bank of Wales. At last I had the breakthrough I'd been looking for. They were very helpful but some of the directors were away from the office until Monday so they could not authorise the deal until then. Back in Worcester, on the Friday, I worked out a plan to delay completion until the following Wednesday. Late Friday I telexed Delglo (no emails then!) six questions which I said I needed answers to satisfy the bank. Barclays had not asked for them but they were entirely relevant. The hope was that they would not reply until sometime on Monday which would be too late for us to go to London.

The plan worked. Late Monday afternoon, I had a furious Mr Dalgliesh on the telephone: "Cecil, I'm trying not to lose my temper. You were supposed to be here in London at 10.30 this morning and you weren't ... and I haven't heard a word from you since. You sent up your financial man to Clay Cross without an agreement, you weren't entitled to do that. We sent him packing. Where were you? Have you got the money?" I said how sorry I was, and that I had been waiting for an answer to my six telexed questions, having assumed they would want to answer them before we met. So I didn't go to London. I knew they had a board meeting on the Tuesday, so that when I suggested being there on the Tuesday morning he said that wasn't convenient – they had a board meeting. Could I be there on the Wednesday morning? I said yes, of course, I'd be there.

"10.30am?"

"Yes, 10.30, no problem."

"And will you have the money?"

"Yes, I'll have the money."

"Right, Cecil, I believe you. We'll see you in London on Wednesday morning."

On the Tuesday I managed to get an agreement with the Bank of Wales in principle, but not a cheque. I spoke to Peter Walker, who offered to give Barclays a call. I assume he did, although I don't know; but suddenly Barclays rang me and said they would deliver the cheque for £350,000 to

With my mother Jean in Ilfracombe in 1952

At my sister Myrtle's wedding in 1958 (Sheila on left)

Beatrice and me on our wedding day
16 September 1961

First factory: the Old Vinegar Works, Worcester

Demonstrating the 'Firefly' in 1970 with Colin Brooks (standing, far right)

Carden Street works, Worcester, 1964

Navigation Road factory, Diglis, opened by Peter Walker MP in 1968

Peter Walker and me at the factory in Worcester

Testing the first combi-boiler in 1970:
(L-R) Ken Waldren, John Stallard and David Steed

Fire destroys the factory in Worcester: July 8 1983

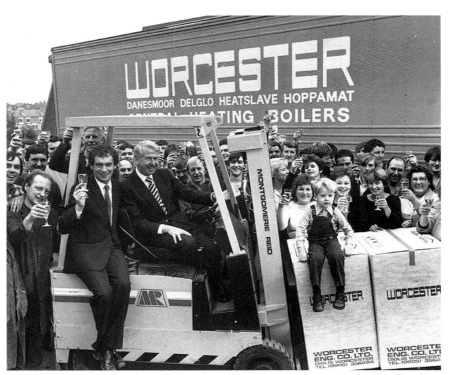

Peter Walker reopens the Diglis factory after the fire.
His son Robin (now MP for Worcester) is sitting on the packing case

The first Heatslave following the fire in 1983

Beatrice and I at Mrs Thatcher's reception at 10 Downing Street for
Britain's most successful entrepreneurs in 1982. Shirley Wickens right.
(Crown Copyright)

With Beatrice at the opening of the Diglis factory in 1968

Celebrating 25 years of Worcester Heat with Beatrice in 1987

me. The final hitch was how I would get hold of the cheque itself. In the end Barclays said they would arrange for us to collect it from a branch near the Delta offices. Nigel Collis and I set off early to London. The bank was not open so we rang the bell as arranged and the cheque was handed over. We were at the Delta office by 10.30am. The financial director asked me if I had the cheque. I said, "Yes, I have, but I'm not going to show it to you until we've concluded the deal". Two hours later we did conclude the deal and I handed it over.

Ironically Barclays then decided they didn't need the mortgage on the factory after all, but after three days trudging round London trying to find the cash I was not in a mood to say thank you very much and abandon my commitment to the Bank of Wales.

We then had to deal with the reality of now owning the factory at Clay Cross. Delglo had been unionised. Worcester never was because we had grown from just me, virtually one person at a time; I had selected everyone, and we were a kind of family. Nevertheless there were some good people at Clay Cross, including the manager, Kevin Lee. We immediately got on well together. As well as Kevin Lee, Clay Cross employed Richard Soper, and David Hall. All three were to become directors of Worcester and play a significant part in the company's development. Kevin stayed on to manage Clay Cross for a number of years and then moved to Worcester to become Manufacturing Director and then, when I retired, he became Managing Director. Naturally there was some apprehension in the workforce. I assured them that we were going to increase the work at the Clay Cross factory. We said we would not only move our Worcester oil-fired boiler production there but also the Delglo boiler manufacturing currently carried out at the Blackpool factory, which hadn't been part of the sale. We also changed the name of the Worcester Firefly boiler to Danesmoor – the name of the Clay Cross boiler. This was for two reasons: one, the change would reassure the new workforce, then around 150 people, that Worcester Engineering was not going to abandon it; and two, Delglo had obviously taken a long view after the Yom Kippur war in 1973 because for the following two years they had heavily promoted their range of Danesmoor boilers. I assume their thinking was that this would give them the potential of being market leaders in oil-fired boilers once the market returned. Obviously they were not able to realise that possibly due to the chairman deciding to sell all the loss-making companies. It wasn't without some sadness that I made that decision. Firefly went back to our beginning.

Delglo, when we took over, was losing money on every boiler they made. We began a major redesign at our development department in Worcester, and within nine months of the acquisition we were able to launch the new unit at an exhibition in London. The previous managing director visited our stand and said what we had done in nine months would have taken Delta three years. I said we had to do it: it was a question of necessity because we couldn't afford the losses.

So we were back on the road, swiftly transforming the Clay Cross operation from loss making to profitability. There was some bluff involved. At times it was like playing a hand of poker. And it wasn't just when trying to buy Delglo; Clay Cross, after all, was an old mining area, and the factory was strongly unionised. Occasionally they sent people down to hand out union leaflets at the Worcester factory but as far as I remember they had no uptake – not one. Nevertheless, despite their working conditions being improved by harmonising with those in Worcester, and giving every worker permanent injury or illness insurance after four years with Worcester – they never agreed the annual salary increase. In Worcester it had never been an issue. We tried to be progressive and pay a reasonable increase relative to the cost of living increases and any increase in productivity, and then gave whatever might seem right – two percent, five per cent perhaps – and come up with a figure that we felt we could afford and enable us to remain competitive. Our employees in Worcester accepted that if that's what the company could afford, that's what they were going to get.

Clay Cross was different. The annual wage increase was awarded at Christmas. From the union at Clay Cross the response was always a formal 'failure to agree' and a refusal to work overtime. It didn't matter too much at first, because that time of the year tended to be quieter than the rest of the year. It was a matter of cash flow and storage; we had to read the market according to the weather. People often don't think about their boiler until the last minute. However, after a couple of years of this mild union intransigence there was a particularly cold snap during October which increased demand. This meant that we needed to work overtime during January and February so we didn't want the usual overtime ban. I suggested to Kevin Lee that he might let the unions know that if they recommended yet another overtime ban I would never offer them overtime again. The tactic worked. I didn't know if it would – you never do. But we never had any problems with the unions after that, at least – not at Clay Cross. That was to come when we tried to take over the Government's co-operative – Kirby Manufacturing and Engineering.

8

Union Power

1978 was a turbulent year for the country. It was to end with the Winter of Discontent, the culmination of the industrial strife that had dogged Britain since the end of the Second World War. James Callaghan's Labour government saw the country called 'the sick man of Europe'. And one of the reasons was encapsulated in our involvement with a Merseyside workers' co-operative that had about ten per cent of the central heating radiator market.

The huge manufacturing plant in Kirby had long been a centre of controversy in the new town. It had had a succession of owners and in 1972 was making washing machines for Fisher-Bendix. Threatened with closure, it became the centre of a celebrated nine week sit-in by its 600 workers under the glare of the media spotlight. The sit-in ended in victory for a charismatic convenor of the Transport and General Workers Union, Jack Spriggs, who persuaded Tony Benn, Industry Secretary in Harold Wilson's Labour government, to back the workers with an investment of £3.9 million of public money. The factory was relaunched as Kirby Manufacturing and Engineering (KME), making various products, including central heating radiators.

By 1977 it had received over £5 million in state aid and had never made a profit. The government, now led by James Callaghan, decided it could no longer keep bailing out the co-operative. The Department for Industry developed a plan for a subsidiary of Metal Box, Stelrad, to take over KME, although it required it to go into voluntary liquidation as a prerequisite. The two KME leaders, Jack Spriggs and Dick Jenkins, were to be sacked. It was supposed to be a secret plan, but it didn't stay secret for long, and Stelrad found itself targeted as a sort of bogeyman.

Radiators were big business, and very simple: basically, two steel panels pressed together. The complicated bit is that you need to produce a whole range of different sorts and sizes to suit people's individual rooms. I went over to Switzerland to look at the latest technology in their radiator manufacturing. The machine they demonstrated to me was about 50 metres long. At one end there was a large roll of sheet steel that was fed automatically forward and formed, cut to length, welded and tested so that a complete radiator arrived at the other end. It was all computer controlled and only required three operators. I was very impressed. Stelrad, who had originally been in the frame to take over KME, was a very successful company with all this latest Swiss technology, but they tended to concentrate on the few major distributors. The market wasn't over saturated and I felt we could fulfill demand. We knew how much investment was needed, we knew how to make a radiator, and we could spend money on production instead of over-manning and waste. By November 1978 KME had virtually run out of cash, despite a government handout in October of another £150,000 to tide the company over while they found a buyer for the company. The Prime Minister, James Callaghan, had, I believe, come to the conclusion that Tony Benn's co-operative just did not work and appointed a much more pragmatic Industry Secretary, Eric Varley, who declared the co-operative had to be sold to private industry.

As a result we put in a request to the Department of Industry to consider a bid by Worcester Engineering to take over the co-operative. A working party was set up to advise the government on the future of KME and came out in favour of our bid. We would receive £4 million from the government, to which we would add a further £4 million. By this time, KME needed around £1.8 million immediately to pay off all its accumulated debts and overdraft. Our bid was subject to negotiation. We believed the government definitely wanted to get rid of KME and there was probably a lot more money around than the £4 million they had put on the table. We had researched the market and had been assured by a number of merchants that they would take the KME radiators if we owned the company. We had also been assured by Stelrad that if we were successful in acquiring KME and wanted to sell it at any time, they would be very interested. I had become a personal friend of Stelrad's MD, Rodney Haynes, so I knew he was a man of his word.

Armed with three facts: (1) there was going to be a lot of government money about so the government could extricate themselves from an impossible situation; (2) the market for the product was there and (3) we had the assurance from Stelrad that if we wanted to sell we were selected to take over KME, I began talks with the men from the ministry. Our plan was to virtually halve the workforce while investing in the new technology, with the help of a government gift amounting to some £4 million. And we made it a requirement that Jack Spriggs and Dick Jenkins were not to be part of the management team. But I began to understand something about union power: it believed in job protection. The unions didn't want to know that technology could reduce the workforce so that those individuals could then go on and do something else – something useful. I started to get letters from employees of KME wishing me success, but pointing out that it would be very difficult. I remember one said of previous attempts: "The common factor in all of them was the role of the shop stewards. They welded the gates to prevent the previous firm from getting in before taking it over themselves. I hope you can think of some way of circumventing them."

Another talked about vehicles arriving in the middle of the night, taking radiators away. I'd heard people say that the plant was jinxed, but at the outset I'd had a lot of admiration for the people there: they'd fought for their jobs and weren't afraid to take on the responsibility of running a workers' co-operative. And they'd shown they could make a good product. The problem was they did not believe in productivity or investment in the product.

The atmosphere, when we went up to meet the workforce at Kirby, was not just cool, but hostile. During that meeting one of their negotiating team said to me: "Some people out there think you're the Messiah, Mr Duckworth, come to save us. But I don't, I think you're the devil." We realised pretty quickly that we had been entirely set up by Jack Spriggs and his colleagues.

Jack Spriggs was quite a character. He had charm and charisma but he and his cohort of fellow shop stewards made me think irresistibly of Peter Sellars in the film *I'm Alright Jack*. How Tony Benn could possibly imagine Jack Spriggs and his colleagues could run a successful business I will never know. What they were good at was going to watch Liverpool play football in the European Cup. Liverpool was in its heyday of cup football and Jack Spriggs and his colleagues were off, I was told, 'looking to buy new machinery' in Moscow or Barcelona or Milan - wherever Liverpool was playing in the Cup.

The problem was that Jack didn't believe they would not get any more cash from the government. Every time they had been back previously, they had come away with the money. Although they had been told this was absolutely their last chance, Jack Spriggs had convinced most of the workforce that he would simply ring up Wedgie Benn who would create something to get them out of the fix. I was astonished that there was no monitoring of how KME was progressing.

I had realised we weren't going to win when Jack called the entire workforce to the canteen one afternoon where he had set up a telephone and a microphone on the stage at one end. "We've been told by the minister that Worcester Engineering is going to take over," he announced. "I'm here to tell you that it isn't going to happen. We got rid of Stelrad," – cheering – "and we are going to get rid of Worcester," – more cheering. "Today we've got a gentleman coming here with the money to bail us out. It won't be a cheque. He's bringing the money in a suitcase and he'll be here shortly." More cheers, shouts of "Jack's done it again!" Then the telephone rang. "This is it, he's probably just arrived." Jack picked up the telephone, listened, shook his head gravely and then turned to his audience. "I'm sorry, guys, he's missed the bus." Much laughter and more cheering. "Good old Jack... you'll find a way!"

The question then was, how did I get out of this gracefully? I went back to the Government and once again laid down our conditions for the takeover, one of which was the exclusion of Jack Spriggs. I said if they couldn't deliver, I would walk away. And of course they failed. They couldn't get Jack Spriggs to honour anything he said. We were, after all, a very small company. A *Daily Telegraph* leader at the time called us a 'pint-size private company'. But we were profitable and had significant growth prospects. Could we make KME work?

We believed we could have done it. We were offering KME a future. But in the end we withdrew our offer and walked away. On December 6th I sent a telex to Brian Hilton, Assistant Secretary, Industrial Financial Division at Kingsgate House, who was handling the negotiations for the Department of Industry:

> You may be aware that Arthur Money, Roger Tomlinson, Kevin Lee and myself were at KME on Tuesday. We had a long meeting with Spriggs and Jenkins and the negotiating committee and we also saw the nightshift until 3am. On Wednesday we had recovered sufficiently to continue and we spent most of the day talking to the management. We have now without doubt come to the conclusion that we should withdraw and we say this for the following reasons:
>
> 1. We do not have a willing seller, without which in itself we believe the acquisition to be impossible.
> 2. The workforce, in our opinion, have been set against us by Spriggs.
> 3. Spriggs has convinced the workforce that far from failing they have been successful over the last four years and they have actually saved the country £3 or £4 million.

4. The co-operative do not accept any responsibility for our having to make 260 people redundant. It has been conveyed to the workforce that it is entirely our fault and apparently we have been set up as "devils" (I quote). Although we had increased our offer on redundancy up to statutory plus one week's pay for every two years served, this was considered totally inadequate and unacceptable.

5. The co-operative also do not accept that there is overmanning in the radiator department and they wish to continue customs and practices they have developed over the last fourteen years, even if we make a loss, and – I quote – "after all, we have £8 million to play with, why do we have to make a profit?"

6. Spriggs continues to manipulate the workforce and continues to interfere with negotiations which we are holding with creditors etc. He also does not accept that there is a time or money constraint, life is about jobs.

7. We do not believe we could introduce a new automatic radiator line at Kirby within 18 months, which we believe to be necessary to stay competitive. This would be far too soon for them to accept and in our view we would have had too little time to establish ourselves, to eliminate mistrust, to change attitudes and to gain a spirit of co-operation.

8. Spriggs has created hysteria about the very name Stelrad and therefore eliminated the possibility of our being involved with Stelrad.

If Spriggs honoured the commitment to the working party and accepted your decision, and had announced to the workforce that he had failed, that the reality was there was no alternative, that Worcester Engineering would bring prosperity and job security for 460 jobs, that he personally supported the decision and he and Jenkins would do all in their power to assist and wished them to support Worcester, then I believe we would have had a totally different atmosphere and under those circumstances, even with all the difficulties with the redundancy, local constraints etc, those could have been overcome.

We know, however, that this has been far from the reality and in fact quite the reverse has been the case. Even now Spriggs appears to be friendly and co-operative to us, but in the last few days we are aware that he is continuing to be devious and to manipulate the situation away from us. For example, he has told the workforce that I have been adopting a God-like arrogance and that I have stated that I am the Messiah come to save them. He placed copies of your telex on Monday [from the government] on the noticeboards, but completely nullified this by adding a footnote to the effect that they need not take any notice as he was talking to politicians and ministers. He also knows that the management is opposed to the co-operative with Worcester Engineering. He tells you on Monday that we have offered them jobs which he knows not to be true, and yet at the same time he is trying to turn the management against us by saying that we have told him that we only intend to employ them for three months and then we will get rid of them, which again is not true.

I had arranged meetings with [bank and our solicitors] today, both of which I have now cancelled, and I apologise if you feel we have let you down. However, with all the goodwill, all the tenacity and all the sincerity in the world, I could not put this company at risk by acquiring KME. We are immensely disappointed and feel very grieved that one man is standing in the way of 460 jobs.

Jack Spriggs believed he was right and it was impossible to change that belief. He was, without doubt, an inspirational leader. Much later, he said all the effort had been worthwhile, with jobs being preserved in a period when employment was very hard to find. His ideology of job protection was in fact quite the reverse. It meant that companies that did not invest in the latest production machinery and were therefore overmanned would be uncompetitive. Radiators would then be imported from Europe. His concept was that you should always have the same number of people doing the same job, and if you think about that for a moment you realise we wouldn't have come out of the Dark Ages if we'd followed that doctrine. At KME all the money was wasted. The plant was behind in terms of technology, efficiency and management. They hadn't invested in the product – or the people, for that matter. And you could see, as is always the danger, that the revolutionaries had adopted a different role for themselves – hence the trips to the Liverpool football matches.

Jack Spriggs went on to be a full-time official of the TGWU and was elected as a member of Liverpool City Council in 1991. In 2002 he served as the city's Lord Mayor and when he died in December 2009 he was much mourned. There were many tributes to him as a 'true gentleman', 'a giant of politics'. The Labour leader of the city council described him as 'an inspiration to everyone... He lived to serve his community and will be remembered for his huge generosity of spirit'. That is not my view. He cost a lot of people jobs and a future. Products that could have been made in the area are now imported from Europe. Unfortunately union power, far from protecting jobs, did the reverse. Indeed I believe that the abuse of union power in the 1960s and 70s is the reason why we have a very much reduced manufacturing industry in the UK today.

KME went bankrupt and the plant was eventually sold to a private sector company, with more subsidies, before it finally closed.

The irony was that for us, 1978 was a very good year. We were turning over £4.7 million with profits now at £350,000. We were gradually becoming cash rich as against borrowing money from the bank. We were paying off our mortgage with the Bank of Wales and sales of the Heatslave were increasing. In fact, we needed more space to expand; we had a small showroom but we wanted a bigger one to demonstrate our products and convince people that we really were the way forward. And we needed more office space. I decided to ask two architects to submit plans for a new office building.

One submission was straightforward; the other was futuristic, all curves and made out of steel. That was the one we went for. It had real impact, and we thought it best portrayed what we were all about – doing something different, something new. It had virtually no straight walls, so it wasn't easy to fix things like pictures or equipment to them, and it was a bit cold in the winter and too hot in the summer, but it was an expression of our faith in the future. The architect was Sid Glazzard of Worcester, and when the building was nearly finished he came to me and said he wanted to talk about the paintwork. The steel roof girders were all visible, and Sid wanted to paint them bright green. The doors would all be brown, with red handles. I said I'd got to live with it every day and I didn't think I could, but he pleaded with me. He promised me I would be pleasantly surprised when it was done and even said he would repaint it if I didn't like the result. I capitulated, and surprisingly enough we did get to like it. For him, it was the finishing touch to his masterpiece, and I realized that in his world, unlike mine, some of the detail simply isn't worked out beforehand - even whether it might leak or not. Decisions like that are made on the hoof, sorted out as they go along. It might be the artistic way, but it did sell the image of being progressive.

I also incorporated a small directors' dining room, chiefly for visitors from other companies, but also because it provided an opportunity for our own directors to meet together and talk about the issues of the day. We were all very busy and rarely got together. However I made a rule that we had to be there by 1.15pm and we would not stay in the dining room one minute after 2pm. That was because we didn't want our employees saying: "Oh, they're in there enjoying themselves". If we wanted to continue a discussion, we had to move out of the dining room so that the staff could see we had emerged, and we would move to someone's office. There was no alcohol, and no one would go out to lunch unless there were very exceptional circumstances – visitors didn't take any of us out to lunch, they came to us. It meant, too, that visitors tended to meet the team, not just the individual with whom they had made the appointment; I always made sure that everybody knew when we had a visitor and made a point of being in the dining room. We had a very good cook – too good, really, we all started putting on weight. But it worked well: it meant we all talked to each other, and if there were little issues, which do develop however apparently trivial, they tended to evaporate over lunch, and we could discuss the problems of the day in a civilized way instead of in the corridor.

The new showroom was not only larger than the old one, but included a lecture room. We were now not only able to demonstrate how we manufactured our boilers and the principles behind the design, but give people the chance to test a working model and see it in action. Then they could visit the factory. I remember one of the leading merchants watching such a demonstration and saying: "This can't be right, you've got some secret pipework here..." We proved that was not the case – the tiny boiler was producing all the hot water flowing from the tap.

In 1979 Peter Walker returned to open the new building. The sun shone on our shiny new building, the Severn sparkled, and the air was full of optimism. Perhaps, I reflected, this was the time to think about going public. Was it the moment to look at something new? Yet there were some clouds on the horizon of the approaching decade. The Ayatollah Khomeini had declared Iran an Islamic republic, following the fall of the Shah in 1978. The price of oil was once more increasing. Were there further squalls ahead?

9

New Horizons

The late 1970s and the 1980s were to be turbulent years, with the miners' strike, a Wall Street crash, famine and bombings, ending with the fall of the Berlin Wall. For us it began with a frisson of alarm when OPEC quadrupled the price of oil between 1979 and 1980. Once again the oil-fired sector of the central heating industry suffered a setback. However we were now getting volume sales through the Heatslave, our gas-fired mains fed combination boiler, so we weren't as dependent on oil. Britain was not on the Iranian embargo list. Nevertheless it did seem sensible to look again at the solid fuel market, still the alternative in many rural areas.

There was already a successful company selling solid fuel boilers: Trianco, whose origins went back to Sheffield in the 1850s and a partnership between a businessman called George Newton and an ironmaster, Thomas Chambers. They developed one of the greatest heavy industrial companies in England, Newton Chambers. Its skills included mining, smelting and casting iron. It built blast furnaces and coke ovens and cast the iron for Tower Bridge. In the early 1970s it acquired a small boiler manufacturer called Trianco Stewart which became Trianco.

Solid fuel boilers were nothing like as good as oil or gas-fired units; they were dirty and dusty and less efficient, but Trianco had virtually no competition and we thought we could design one that was rather better. We called it the Hoppamat. It was launched in 1980 and was manufactured at Clay Cross. Within twelve months it was selling pretty well. Then, out of the blue, Trianco declared that we had infringed their patent on their own solid fuel boiler.

We knew the patent was out of date, and we also knew that although some aspects of the Hoppermat were similar to Trianco's boiler – after all, theirs was the only one on the market – we had also changed a lot of things and improved it considerably. We were also confident that the Trianco boiler was comfortably outside the patent protection period. It was: but then we were accused of infringing not the patent, but the copyright on Trianco's engineering drawings.

Copyright law is, and always has been, a matter of infinite interpretation. Patent law itself has been confused with copyright protection. I thought it was complete nonsense to say that we had infringed Trianco's copyright on the *drawings* – since when had engineering drawings been subject to copyright? However, I then discovered that the penalties for transgressing a copyright were far more onerous than for breaking a patent. Damages incurred by infringing copyright could amount to a significant percentage of a company's turnover. I realised this was serious. We could be crippled if the case was proved. And production would have to be halted immediately.

So I found myself in the arcane and labyrinthine world of the law. I consulted a patent law specialist, of course, and was told that there was confusion over copyright and patent law but we could be 75% certain of success if we fought the case. Unfortunately, as we came closer and closer to the day of the trial at the High Court in the Strand, so that percentage diminished until it reached 50-50. Is this a common experience? I had no idea, but as I walked through Lincoln's Inn to our barrister's chambers I began to wonder if it wasn't all something of a legal game. That impression was not helped by our barrister's preference for having his name pronounced 'Fyshe' despite being spelt Fish.

The trial didn't do a great deal to increase my respect for the workings of the law. The judge's expertise was in tax, not copyright, and I don't think he ever understood the difference between patent law and copyright. And engineering drawings had been given copyright protection by another judge who was presumably a sound and honourable man but unaware of the implications of his judgment. So absurd was the situation that a few years later engineering drawings ceased to be included in copyright law, but we were just caught in that brief time frame. By day three of the trial I was not impressed by the fact that the judge appeared to be fast asleep, although at the debrief in chambers afterwards Mr Fish seemed quite excited by the fact that he had looked up on one occasion. He concluded that we had had a good day, although I found it difficult to understand quite why.

That evening I had a call from my lawyer. He said the opposition was prepared to settle out of court. I said: "I thought we were going to win this? Why should we settle?"

"We could win it, but what happens if we lose?"

"That has certainly occurred to me," I said.

"Well," said my lawyer, "if you take my advice, you will settle."

It was going to cost us £150,000 and that was a lot of money to me. I said I'd think about it, and he said we had to let them know by 9 o'clock that evening. After some discussion we did settle, because we would then be able to continue selling the Hoppermat. The case was abandoned and we never knew if we could have won it or not. Much later one of Trianco's directors said he had nothing personal against us, but he thought they might make some money out of the case and it would help them to brush us aside, but the advice had been that they should settle. As I had never really believed solid fuel had a future, particularly as the oil price was now coming down, it wasn't long before we discontinued the Hoppamat. For us the Hoppermat was only ever intended to be a product which filled a gap in the short term. In any case, we were concentrating on our combination boiler. The potential of getting the water bylaws and building regulations changed in our favour was now much closer, and we embarked on a single minded development programme. The first thing we needed was a modulating gas valve so that the boiler would have a range from nine kilowatts for central heating to 24 kilowatts for domestic hot water.

One of the leaders in the field was Honeywell, a company that had grown from its United States origins into an international group. One of its European subsidiaries was in the Netherlands, and it was there that I went to see the Technical Director. I explained how we had so far circumvented the water bylaws but that we now foresaw being able to connect the boiler directly to the mains within the next few years. His response was encouraging: "Thank God for someone enlightened in this country. I've been telling other manufacturers for years that the combination boiler will come."

"Well, don't tell them anymore," I said.

Honeywell had not yet made a modulating gas valve, but they had a prototype in their development department in Amsterdam. Following my visit to see it, I decided to place an order for one – the first one – and told the technical director I would prefer that they didn't supply it to any of the other manufacturers for twelve months. That would give us a lead. He agreed, and we had a gentleman's agreement that he would not sell the new valve until we were out in the marketplace with our new boiler. Later they put up a little plaque at Honeywell in the Netherlands, commemorating Worcester Engineering's first order of a modulating gas valve.

The next thing we needed was a copper heat exchanger, instead of cast iron. At one of the Paris exhibitions I found an Italian manufacturer who had produced a prototype and was just about to go into production. Frustratingly, the government was still moving very slowly on changing the water bylaws so we still had to put a 'heat bank' alongside the heat exchanger, which made the boiler bigger and heavier and rather more expensive. But the heat bank meant we could use a standard gas valve, enabling us to produce a wall-hung boiler with a lightweight heat exchanger. It was not an ideal solution, but it did increase sales and further establish the combi concept. Wall-mounted units were dominating the market and at least we were now able to compete in this expanding sector. We called the new boiler the 'Heatslave Junior' and were surprised at just how successful it was. It was another indication that a fully modulating combi would be a massive hit.

In 1982, I was selected as one of the leading entrepreneurs in the country. The word 'entrepreneur' wasn't in common use then. Beatrice and I were invited to meet Margaret Thatcher at No. 10 Downing Street. We were allowed two extra people so I took two of my longest serving employees: David Jones and Shirley Wickens. Our visit coincided with crucial talks on the Falklands crisis, the war between Britain and Argentina having suddenly erupted that spring. There was understandable doubt as to whether our meeting with Mrs Thatcher would even take place, but she apparently said no, she would not postpone it: "I do want to see these people... They are very important".

When we entered Downing Street it was thronged with people, and as we arrived at No. 10 a Cabinet meeting had just finished and we walked up past people like Lord Hailsham and Michael Heseltine, journalists parting to allow us through. We felt very important. We entered No. 10 and were invited upstairs to meet Mrs Thatcher. We talked about Worcester, and what we were doing, and she was very interested – it was a great occasion.

It was in that year that we began to look ahead to expansion in other fields beyond the boiler industry. I talked to my colleagues about the possibility of becoming a public company, the benchmark for which was to achieve a target of £1 million profit in order to float on the stock exchange. Acquisition was one way to achieve it. We were prompted by an approach from a company called Bifurcated which was already on the stock exchange and might provide us with a way on to the market. Bifurcated made industrial fasteners – bolts, rivets etc – and was based in Aylesbury. They were much bigger than us but we were profitable and they were starting to lose money, so the idea was that we would operate a reverse takeover and turn them around. We would have access to the capital markets and become a public company.

In the end I wasn't sure that the plan would work. Bifurcated was essentially in the metal bashing business, and although it had been hugely successful, it didn't require very high technical skills. Industrial fasteners were already coming in from the Far East and we were losing industries like shipbuilding, which used them. I began to wonder if it wouldn't be a millstone round our necks, and concluded that it would. We withdrew from the deal with Birfurcated, but my ambition remained. One of those I talked to about my plans was my old friend John Cornford, whom I had met on my first day at primary school back in Macclesfield. John's father had been in the paper industry and John had joined his father's company when he left school before leaving to become Sales Director of a business making coated papers and board in Manchester. It was called Packaging Products and was a subsidiary of a company called Capseals.

One morning I had a telephone call from John. Would I be interested in a packaging company?

"I would be if I could make a profit," I replied.

"Right. I think our company could be up for sale. There's a bit of work to do, but I just wanted to be sure you would be interested."

Capseals were keen to sell to an American operation, and wanted to get rid of Packaging Products, which was overmanned and making losses despite being one of only about three such companies in the country and having a pretty good order book. Armed with John's discreet inside information, I went to see the chairman of Capseals at his London flat to express an interest in acquiring Packaging Products. He was understandably suspicious because he knew that I knew John Cornford. What he perhaps didn't know was that anyone else who came to look at the company would naturally meet John, who might just have been persuaded to put them off a little. As Sales Director, John was in the unique position of having been given the task of selling the company. There was a team of four directors who had worked up a plan of survival which involved dropping all the loss making operations and making 150 people redundant out of a workforce of 210.

There were key issues which we had to satisfy: firstly, could we be certain that the unions would honour an agreement for 150 people to take redundancy? Secondly, could we keep the tax losses, which would enable us to make savings of around £320,000, which was more than the price we were to offer Capseals for the business? Could the company become profitable?

The management team consisted of the Managing Director, Ken Hayes who was very capable but nearing retirement; Brian Elton, the Finance Director and also very capable; Tony Bennett, the Operations Director, very creative and an excellent manager; and John Cornford, the Sales Director who I knew I could trust with my life. They were a good team so if they believed they could run a profitable business with 60 employees it was a calculated risk worth taking, providing the union could deliver. Brenda Dean who headed up the SOGAT print union in the North West was fortunately a progressive and realistic lady and someone we could trust.

After considering these factors we decided to put in a bid of £300,000 for the company. Capseals agreed our terms and we acquired the business.

To mark the signing of the deal John Cornford gave up smoking and he has never smoked since. Packaging Products went on to make a profit of £300,000 in its first year. Subsequently we actually sold the company to John, and now three of his four sons run it, the head office still being in Manchester. To have reached such a culmination of our school life together was very satisfying.

1982 was a year of acquisitions. Once more we were approached by a company in some difficulty. Metal Construction Ltd (MCL) was a Worcester construction engineering company that was losing about £100,000 a year and struggling with its bank. But they had some good contracts and they were very sound engineers, among them the technical director Brian Wilkes who I had first met many years earlier when Beatrice and I used to go to watch Worcester Rugby at Bevere. Brian was a very good scrum half as well as being a good engineer. In those days scrum halves used to fling the ball out, body and all, and as a result Brian does not walk too well these days. I liked what I saw of the company and knew that we could make a real difference. Again, like John Cornford, I knew Brian Wilkes was not only a very good engineer but someone I could trust. We gave MCL confidence. Our success appeared to be infectious. Instead of spending most of their time wondering if they were going to survive, they could spend all their energy doing what they were good at.

MCL had hitherto relied on word of mouth and the continuity of orders from consultants who knew them. We produced brochures which told people what they did and made sure that their expertise was well advertised. In its first year with us, MCL made a profit of about £200,000, a considerable turnaround. We were also able to move our welding team to MCL to give them the benefit of greater output in relation to the size of their operation, and release space for our expanding fabrication of gas boilers. Neither MCL nor Packaging Products were going to be part of our long term strategy but, in the short term, they were profitable. Packaging Products' annual profit was soon to reach £500,000 and a few years later MCL's profits hit a high of over £1,000,000.

There was one sobering revelation in our acquisition of MCL. One of the financial people, whom everyone trusted, appeared one Saturday morning at a bank in Pershore where the managing director's daughter happened to be doing some relief work. She knew him, naturally enough; had a brief chat, and subsequently mentioned to her father that she had seen 'Mr W' cashing a cheque. He thought no more of it until something made him wonder why he should be cashing a cheque at all. On investigation it emerged that 'Mr W' had been exploiting a system in the construction business called 'snagging' – the process of identifying defects. Small amounts could be claimed for resolving these defects. By changing a letter in the title of one of the companies making such claims, 'Mr W' had managed to take several thousand pounds a year out of MCL. His colleagues were devastated to discover that while the company was making losses, 'Mr W' was making a small private fortune.

Apart from that, MCL was another successful step towards my goal of going public and thereby expanding both in the UK and abroad. Not that every purchase was quite so rewarding – indeed, I think I might have got a little carried away, because I then pursued a company called Morgan Air. It was a Birmingham company which made ducting systems for industrial ventilation and heating, and as it appeared to have a large order book and a long list of debtors I thought we could turn the company round. Well, we didn't: but I learned a few lessons along the way, not the least of which was just how difficult that kind of sub-contracting business can be. Morgan Air might have appeared to have a long list of debtors, but actually collecting those debts was a very different matter. In such a situation you find yourself almost wholly dependent on the main contractor agreeing that the debt was genuine, and it didn't matter if the architect or the structural engineer had got it wrong – you are the one who ends up bearing the cost. There is a constant conflict. As the sub-contractor you have little power against the main contractor.

I also learned something about negotiating. I thought I was a reasonable negotiator, but the managing director of Morgan Air was almost impossible. I would ask him questions, only to receive no answer at all: he was simply silent. Wondering if he had heard at all, and driven to not only repeat the question but following it with "Well... any comments?" he would eventually reply simply, "I'm listening". As a result we christened him 'I'm listening'.

I had deviated from the golden rule: don't go into an area you know little or nothing about. In retrospect we must have got carried away with our success with Packaging Products and MCL; not only did we know nothing about the contract world, we did not know the management team. Luck was with us, nevertheless, because although we didn't make a profit on Morgan Air we did sell the factory to our next door neighbour in Birmingham, who wanted to expand and was keen to buy the site. That resulted in us not losing money after taking the sale of the property into account.

By the beginning of 1983 the Junior Heatslave was selling well. At the factory in Diglis and at Clay Cross we were working virtually a six day week. I didn't want to have to work Sundays on a regular basis because people do get tired, and productivity goes down rather than up if too many hours are worked. Nevertheless a lot of overtime was being worked and it became obvious that the factory was too small. I had been able to lease an adjacent factory about 300 yards away for the fabrication department, but I was looking into buying some more land at Diglis. Perhaps it was just as well that I hadn't been able to. If I had, we would have been committed to Diglis and it was always going to be too small. So perhaps some luck was still with us, even if disaster was about to strike out of a clear blue summer sky.

10

Ashes

Friday, July 8th 1983, was a beautiful day. The sun was sparkling on the river and there was a shimmer of heat over the water meadows. I could hear the bing-bong of an ice cream van. There was a feeling of summer holidays in the air: the factory was approaching its annual shut down. Beatrice and I were looking forward to going to the Ludlow Festival with Nigel and Linda Collis that evening, to see *The Taming of the Shrew*. Shakespeare was performed in the open air, within the massive castle ruins. Picnics and champagne were the usual thing...

I was in my office with the production manager, Clive Perry, discussing whether or not we should work on the Saturday. We had the orders, but did we have all the components we needed; which sections should be asked to do the overtime? It was also the day before the works' annual shutdown. And then I heard the fire alarm.

At first I thought it was a practice. But it kept going. Finally I said: "Well, we might go and take a look, it's been going for some time."

It wasn't a practice. People were unreeling fire hoses. I could see smoke coming from the paint plant. Black smoke. Somebody was triggering a fire extinguisher. Everyone was forming a circle, watching. And then, all at once, just above the spray booth, a huge ball of fire seemed to explode out of the roof of the paint plant and career across it, like a tsunami of flame (I learned subsequently that when the insulation material in the roof reaches a certain temperature, it ignites at a rate of 100 feet a second). Everybody was running for their lives as the flames billowed across the factory. At that moment, I remember thinking: "Well, that's blown working tomorrow..." Followed by, "God... how are we going to resolve *this* problem?"

Fire engines were arriving. David Steade from the development department had been across the road in a builders' merchants buying some screws or something when the assistant glanced past him and said: "Is that smoke coming from your building, or is it from behind?" David looked over his shoulder. "That's us..."

He ran back, told the receptionist to turn off the electricity, set the fire alarm off and telephone the fire service. People inside the factory were quite unaware of the huge plumes of smoke pouring out: the fire had ignited inside the ducting in the paint plant, and they were still merrily spraying away while the fire built up above them and the heat intensified by the second. Paint had built up inside the ducting and the motor had shorted.

I met the first fire engine as it arrived on the scene. It was, as these things are, almost unreal: I could see it all happening in front of my eyes, and yet the horror seemed to have suspended time. Was it really happening?

"Where's the fire hydrant?" a fireman asked... and I thought, stupidly perhaps, well, you're the fireman, you should know. As it happened, I did know, because the fire hydrant had played a central role at every stag night by having the future bridegroom tied to it, sometimes for rather longer than intended. So I knew exactly where it was. "There it is - carry on," I said, even then with a kind of naïve belief that they would soon have it out, now they had arrived. However I began to grasp very quickly that they wouldn't. The fire was already raging in the factory. Nigel Collis realised we had to rescue all the computer disks from the offices in case the fire destroyed all our data... There was no shortage of volunteers and they managed to get everything out through the windows.

Eventually there were about 13 fire engines fighting the blaze and they were running out of water - they couldn't get enough out of the hydrant. They had to get pipes laid down to the River Severn, about 400 yards away and it seemed to take for ever to get them all connected up... and all the time the fire was raging out of control, black smoke and flames rising and coiling into the sky, devouring the factory. I said to the fire chief: "When do you think you're going to get this out?" He replied simply: "It'll be a long time, sir. The factory's gone." If I recall those words, it still brings a lump to my throat. At the time I couldn't speak for ten minutes. It was one of the worst moments of my life.

The fire chief was still speaking: "I think we've just got to try and save the offices. Now, tell me - any hazardous stuff in there?"

There were, of course, oxygen and acetylene bottles in the factory. A lot. If they were to explode it would be like a bomb going off. We drew a diagram to show where they were, so that the firemen would be able to locate them and get them out. If the bottles fractured in the heat... The fire fighters were incredibly brave, wearing oxygen masks and crawling on their bellies into that inferno of flame and smoke, always aware what could happen at any second. It could have been the end of any or all of them. But they did get all the gas bottles out; although very distorted by the heat, they were still intact. We were safe at least from that threat. It was an amazing feat by those brave firemen.

Eventually they got the fire under control, although they said they would be around for a long time to make sure. There was nothing more I could do there. I drove home then, washed and shaved; I had agreed with Nigel that we might as well go to the open air theatre in Ludlow. I had rung Beatrice so she knew all about the fire. It was a lovely evening and she thought it would be a good idea to go, so we went. I rather wish the play had been *Much Ado About Nothing*, it might have raised a smile... as it was I don't think I remember anything about *The Taming of the Shrew*. My mind simply went round and round, thinking, how the hell do we get out of this. I had the curious feeling that I was slowly losing an arm or something, that I had no control over what was happening. I had read somewhere that statistically only one out of three companies survives a major fire, which didn't help. Everything had been going so well – we were busier than we had ever been. We had had setbacks before, but this was so sudden, so completely out of the blue.

The next morning, that first morning after the fire, I had asked the workforce to meet up at 9am – and everybody was there. It was a scene of complete devastation. The fire brigade people did a wonderful job and were extremely brave, and they did save the offices, but it took a long time to put the fire out and by then there was nothing left of the factory but part of its blackened skeleton. It was made somehow more dreadful by that beautiful July morning, the sun on the black wasteland of what was now simply almost unidentifiable rubbish. You can't imagine steel burning, but it does, it burns and it buckles in that intensity of heat.

Much later someone asked me if I ever thought that was it... that I couldn't go on. Of course it was traumatic. But no, I never thought that. I thought: we can get out of this, we can recover, and I began to set about planning how we would.

The first thing I did was to tell those employees who were already on annual leave that there would a job for them when they came back in two weeks time. Then I asked for volunteers to help clear up the site. The debris was almost all rubbish, but it all had to be got into trucks and taken away to be sorted through. It was amazing. Everybody talks about the Dunkirk spirit, the British character – and it's all true. People not only worked like hell – and it was a kind of hell, they were all soon black with oily soot – but they were almost enjoying it, feeling they were part of something special, which of course they were. The plan was to rebuild the factory, re-equip it and be back in full production in 100 days. Not everyone – well, perhaps no one – shared my confidence, but that was the target.

The first port of call was our insurers. Nigel had renegotiated the terms of our insurance only a few weeks before, so we were neither over nor under insured. We may have been lucky, but one thing you realise in that sort of situation is how crucial that is. We were with Norwich Union, and they were very good in getting assessors on site and agreeing to let us have interim payments. You never know how good your insurance company is until you make a claim. Norwich Union (now Aviva) were VERY good. Then we started ordering new machinery to move back into the leased building we had just vacated. Within four days, some £1.5 million worth of equipment was on its way.

People were working 24 hours a day, seven days a week. The site was cleared in two weeks, and the fortnight's annual shutdown allowed us to get production running again on the leased site. We were back in business. The fire had made the national press as well as the heating industry press, so everybody knew we had had a major fire, but we sent letters to everyone saying that we would have things up and running again in two weeks time. Our competitors may have been quietly gloating, but we had the camaraderie of the workforce as well as the support of merchants around the country who were willing to move stock from, say, Manchester to Sussex to fulfill orders. We had to get their confidence. I rang Peter Walker to tell him what had happened – he was still our MP and close friend, and he came over and said cheerfully, "Well, this time I can come and do the official closure of the factory…"

We did not quite make the 100 days. It took 109 to rebuild the factory. And we now not only had a new factory, but it was newly wired, with new machinery, new pneumatic systems throughout, all of which would be of huge benefit in the years ahead. Once again, we had turned a disaster into a success.

Peter Walker came to open the new factory again. He was accompanied by his young son, Robin, then about five years old and riding on a sack truck. He has since followed his father by becoming MP for Worcester. Everyone in the company had worked tirelessly to get the show back on the road. Peter Walker was a brilliant speaker and, as always, he made everybody involved feel important. It was a new beginning.

We were now an experienced team, all only in our early 40s, who liked working together. I was Managing Director looking after sales, marketing and development in particular. Arthur Money's specific role was to establish our Heatslave mains-fed combi boilers. Our patented unique heatbank unit would have limited appeal. It had three major disadvantages: one, it was too big; two, it was too expensive to produce and three, it was not very responsive. Arthur's job was to help where he could in making these early (Heatbank) combis work more efficiently. That was short term. His main job and focus was to persuade the government to change the building regulations

Roger Tomlinson was the third member of the top team and took the role of Purchasing Director. This involved having available all the different components – steel, copper, paint, etc. at the right price at the right time. Stock control is vital to any manufacturing process. In manufacturing a boiler there are over one hundred different items, some costing one penny, others costing upwards of £40. If one item is missing you cannot complete the boiler. If you have too much stock it can cause massive storage and cash flow problems.

Nigel Collis, our Finance Director, completed the team at that time. Keeping a good grasp on our cost control and producing management accounts accurately and on time is vital and I also worked closely with Nigel when we were considering an acquisition.

In addition to the directors we had some excellent managers. David Steade, who at the time was our Development Manager; Kevin Lee who managed Clay Cross, and Richard Soper who was Sales Manager. Later all became directors of the company. Kevin Lee first became Manufacturing Director and then Managing Director in 1997 when I retired. Richard Soper, the best salesman I have ever met, became Sales and Marketing Director and then Managing Director after Kevin retired in 2001. David Steade became Technical Director in 1990. He was the best in the industry and, working with myself, ensured that our boilers were superior to the competition. We were always one step ahead.

It was a great team and there were others who contributed to our success: Clive Perry, David Jones, Shirley Wickens, Norman Jenkins, Ian Done, Terry Kay and many others.

11

Phoenix

The fire was devastating at the time but, on reflection, we did have some good luck. If we were going to have a fire, midday on a Friday afternoon just before the annual shut-down would be the time to choose. Fortunately we had not sub-let the building we had vacated so we had somewhere to go and owning our own construction company, MCL, meant we could re-build the factory in double quick time. The work force was magnificent and the offices had been saved. We had a new factory with new machinery, the development department and the stores were untouched by the fire as they were housed in a separate building, so not only were we back in business we were ready to fly.

Our oil-fired boilers were selling well. It was a small market but there were fewer manufacturers. And because we had kept our development department going, we were technically in front of our competitors, which resulted in us increasing our market share. The Junior gas-fired Heatslave boilers were also selling well and a change in building regulations was on the horizon. Honeywell had put their modulating gas valve into production. It was now time to redouble our efforts in the development department. Technically we could achieve a range of nine kilowatt to a maximum output of 24 kW. At that time the German sports car manufacturer Porsche had a car called the 9.24 so we thought it would be a good marketing ploy to call our new fully modulating combi a 9.24. The 9.24 was not fully developed. There were almost two years to go before its planned launch date. We were working on a new dry-walled copper heat exchanger and the electronics which would drive the gas modulating valve. The 9.24 would be smaller, only 500mm wide, as against the Junior at 625mm wide and much lighter at below 50 kilos. It would also be much less expensive to produce and much more responsive than the heat bank system we had had to use in the early Heatslaves.

1985 was approaching when the new building regulations would come into force, permitting direct mains hot water. We had frozen the design of the

9.24 and field trials were going well. Knowing when to freeze the design is very important. Being engineers, we knew that given another one or two years it would be possible to produce a better boiler. The problem was that even if the market or the competition would allow us, we would then still want another two years to produce something even better. Those ideas would have to wait and be incorporated in a new 9.24 in, say, three years time. The launch date was approaching and our new brochure and advertising would be hammering home the advantages of a Worcester Combination system against what was, at the time, the conventional British system.

Our plan was to target houses with up to three and four bedrooms (of which there were approximately 25 million in the UK) and convert Britain from a bath-taking nation into shower-taking. As our launch brochure explained:

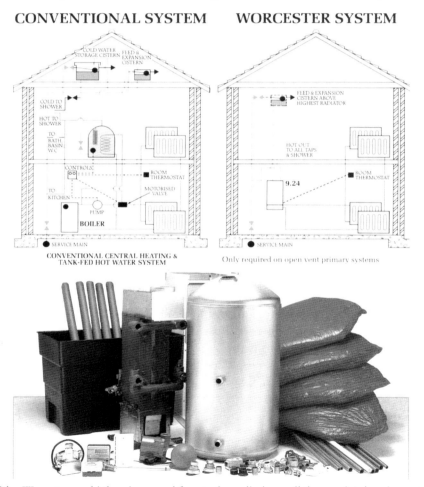

With a Worcester combi there is no need for a tank, a cylinder or all the associated equipment.

Had we got it right when the rest of the industry had got it wrong? We would soon find out!

The 9.24 was immediately successful. We couldn't build enough of them. The indifference, sometimes scepticism, of our competitors turned to grudging interest. Even British Gas began to think there was something in the new concept, the combi boiler. We discovered they had carried out a survey asking people who had invested in our combi boiler what they thought of it; would they have another one, would they recommend it to their friends? The answers were overwhelmingly positive, close on 90%. I knew then that we were indeed ahead of the game. And we knew we had the team to keep on improving. We had new designs in the pipeline. We were using integrated circuit boards to cut out the wiring and getting every component increasingly integrated. And we were making boilers more cheaply. It used to take us about eight man hours to build a boiler in 1983, and our new target was below four, possibly three. We were going to need a bigger factory.

I began to look for land. Finding industrial development land in Worcester wasn't easy, but north of the city, close to Junction 6 of the M5, there were plans for some 70 acres of green field sites in what had once been the rural parish of Warndon to be made available for new industries. We began negotiations with Worcester City Council to buy eleven acres. I wanted to have enough space for a factory building about 200,000 boilers a year – at the time we were building 30,000. So it was pretty ambitious. There was already a Japanese company, Mazak, on site and the council had completed the service roads to provide access on three sides, which was a big advantage. They also completed the link to Junction 6 on the M5 motorway half a mile away.

The British Gas survey confirmed our belief that we were going to be successful. We believed the 9.24 combi would catch the British manufacturers flat footed; they accounted for almost 100% of the market but were all wedded to producing cast iron boilers. British Gas had successfully completed the conversion from town gas to natural gas. Cast iron was no longer necessary. Our combi sales were rocketing. Metal Castings and Packaging Products were increasing their profitability so thought of going public on the London Stock Exchange was a definite option. If we could have access to the capital markets, we would not only have organic growth, we would be able to expand by acquisition.

After much discussion we decided to place shares on what was then known as the Unlisted Securities Market (USM), which came into being in 1980.

It was a vehicle for companies too small for a full listing on the stock exchange and did not require the full year's trading history needed by the main market and could, if they wished, float less than 25 per cent of their share capital. To prepare for going public we decided to make a few changes.

The first change was our name. We had always been Worcester Engineering Limited, but I felt that the future would extend beyond boilers into other associated equipment, for example radiators, showers, etc. I also decided we should separate the operating company from the main group. So we became Worcester Group plc, incorporating the operating side as Worcester Heat Systems. That way we could encompass future acquisitions. We also acquired a distinctive wavy line as our new logo.

The City is not simply a part of London inhabited by bankers, investment managers, accountants and lawyers. It has a kind of life of its own, as if it is some mysterious and powerful being which must be placated. As supplicants for its approval, we had to find new accountants who understood its ways. We were very happy with our local accountants, Rabjohns, but we were told that they would not be accepted. We went to KPMG. We were recommended to a broker who could explain the rules, written or otherwise, by which we had to abide. As a public company we could be vulnerable to criticism over things like cars for our directors' wives. Nothing wrong with that for a private company, but as a public company I felt it might be considered unethical. We had to explain the combi to the City's various analysts, whose natural reaction tended to be curiosity as to why Potterton – or Ideal Standard, or Glow Worm – weren't manufacturing a combi. My reply was: "Well, they will, but they've decided for the moment that it isn't part of their strategy." The City began to like the idea of the combi boiler. If anything, I oversold the concept – although I was simply stating the reality. Nothing was hidden, and the City's checks are meticulous. No doubt it swiftly recognized that with a share of the UK market of less than three per cent, our potential for growth was excellent. Whatever the reason, they bought into the idea in a very big way.

In 1985 our group turnover was running at £15 million and pre-tax profits were over £600,000. 900,000 shares were placed on the USM in May 1986 at a launch price of 110p. We were to become the fastest moving share on the stock market. In just over twelve months the price reached £12.50 and profits had risen to £2.2 million.

I hadn't sold any of my own shares when we went public, but suddenly the brokers were pressurising me to sell at least some of them to give more liquidity to the sales, so great was the demand. I remember sitting at a friend's house reading the *Financial Times*, and of course looking at our share price. It had moved up 50p in a day. And it dawned on me that actually meant £1.5 million *to me*. I thought: I'll sell some shares. Not many, because I wanted to make sure I always retained at least more than 30% of the total equity, which effectively meant keeping control of the company, because it was very difficult for anyone outside to harness the 50% or more required to gain control if I owned 30%.

Through the letterbox dropped a cheque for £1 million. I thought, that wasn't a bad idea. A week later the demand for Worcester Group shares had increased – and so had the selling price. Two weeks later the brokers telephoned to ask if I could sell some more, so I did. A second cheque for just over £1 million arrived in the post. For the first time in my life I was wealthy in real terms, not just on paper. I was just 49. It was a moment to savour.

"What are you going to do with all that money?" friends asked.

I didn't want a new car. The Jensen by now had been supplanted by a Bentley and an Aston Martin. Beatrice and I discussed whether we should move house, but it was impossible to find a comparable site, high on an open hilltop with views to the Malverns. We had 13 acres of land, a large garden, an indoor swimming pool and tennis court and were tucked away off the beaten track within a short drive of Worcester and we had been happy there for 16 years. We did decide to renovate the house and had a lot of enjoyment in drawing up a list of all the things we'd like and realised that with a bit of imagination we could achieve them all. We called in the architect and considerably upgraded the specification to both the house and the swimming pool. It took about a year to complete so we went away rather a lot. Naturally there was quite a bit of disruption but it was worth it.

Then Beatrice said: "Why don't you have a chauffeur?

I thought about it for quite a long time. For someone from a middle class background, who had always been part of a team in which I knew everyone by their first name, I had to go through a bit of a barrier to consider having a chauffeur. And of course with a chauffeur went the appropriate car. I remembered once having breakfast with the legendary Jim Slater who, with Peter Walker, founded a merchant bank called Slater Walker which had been very successful before it collapsed in 1974. I met him for breakfast at Crockfords when he was once again successful, partly through his children's books, and he told me that even during the worst of times he did not want to get rid of his car and his chauffeur, and he'd managed to hang on to them. As we left he went outside ahead of me, and immediately a Rolls Royce glided to the front doorstep. He said, "Take Mr Duckworth to the Hilton Hotel, would you?" and that somehow lived with me. I thought, 'One day...'

As Beatrice pointed out, I could have a telephone in the car so that I could carry on working while travelling – I was driving around the country a lot at the time, talking to merchants, having trade evenings, demonstrating the product, making sure we had the right distribution. It was time-consuming and tiring. I also had to visit investors in London, Glasgow and Edinburgh. So after a lot of thought, I advertised for a chauffeur.

Metal Box had just ceased to supply chauffeurs to their office in Worcester, so I was fortunate in having an answer to my advert from one of them who was looking for a new post. His name was Neville Bladen and he was probably about 55 then, courteous and charming. I was still finding this all a little awkward, so I suggested that as Nigel Collis and I were having to go to London he could drive us as a trial run to see how we'd get on. He appeared next morning in uniform, cap and grey suit and leather gloves and drove us to London and back. I said: "Yes, I would like you to work for me. But you won't need the hat and the gloves as far as I'm concerned. Keep those for the Queen."

A few years later the Queen came to Worcester in connection with the restoration of the cathedral, with which I had been involved. I was to be introduced. And as I went out that morning I saw Neville polishing the Bentley, which by now I had upgraded to a Bentley Continental. He was wearing his cap and grey leather gloves and looked immaculate.

"You are looking very smart today," I said cheerfully. "What's on, Neville?"

He looked at me reproachfully. "It's the Queen today, sir." He had remembered my throwaway line from two years previously. It was a lovely moment.

It was a curious kind of leap for me, having a chauffeur. But I quickly realised what a huge advantage it was. I could work up to the moment we arrived at our destination, and I didn't have to think about time, or parking, or the weather. I understood exactly what Jim Slater had meant.

In October 1987 we moved from the USM to the main stock market. We were making a group profit of over £3 million and were forecast to make over £5 million in 1988. Because a share price of £12.50 was so high for a relatively small company, a three to one issue was organised to make the shares more marketable; there were four times as many shares, but each one was worth a quarter of the previous price. It would be much more flexible. We chose the day when much of southern England was paralysed by the Great Storm, memorably not forecast by Michael Fish, and we had to get dispatch riders to take the papers to the City.

The new factory, too, was going ahead at Warndon. Following Black Monday, 19 May 1987, there were jitters in the City, and subsequent fears of recession made me wonder if we should pull out. But I knew it would cost a lot to withdraw at this stage and recalled that it was often said one should build during a recession. So I thought, that's what I'm going to do. I went ahead, although even more conscious of the size of our investment. The architect had specified large mature trees in the plan for the car parking area which were going to cost about £30,000, so I rang the planners to explain that I would like to change them for small saplings. His reply rather took me aback:

"Mr Duckworth, you can have cutbacks, but not at the expense of the environment."

After a moment I said, "Oh, I thought it was something worth considering."

He went on: "Mr Duckworth, you do know that when you have built the factory you must have satisfied all the planning requirements before we can actually give approval for anyone to work in the factory, or even to open it." I put the phone down and thought – we will see about that!

I was confident that the planners wouldn't stop opening a new factory because the trees in the car park weren't the right size. We built the factory, and we planted small saplings, and never heard any more from the planners. Of course not surprisingly the saplings have now grown into large mature trees.

As planned, in 1988 we introduced a much improved combi 9.24. Other British manufacturers were then also reluctantly introducing combis. It was difficult for them because, firstly they had been rubbishing the concept, and secondly they did not want to give Worcester more credibility. It was also difficult because they really wanted to sell a conventional cast iron boiler. At the time it seemed their marketing strategy was: we don't really want to sell you a combi but if you really want one, why not buy ours. We took advantage of this dilemma. Combis continued to increase their market share and we were in the happy position of increasing our share of the expanding combi market.

The success of the 9.24 also attracted an unlikely possibility in a new market. We were approached by a British company who had successfully completed a number of turnkey operations (new, fully-operational factories producing established products) in Russia. This was before the Berlin Wall came down; Gorbachev was in power and had introduced *perestroika* and *glasnost*. The Russian government believed that they should introduce a gas-fired central heating boiler onto the market and they had engaged a British company they knew and trusted to look for a suitable European boiler and build a factory to produce 100,000 units per year.

They chose the 9.24. Russian engineers arrived in Worcester. We sent samples to Russia and waited for a response. In due course it came: they liked the boiler and wanted the turnkey company to provide detailed costings of the 9.24. They also wanted to know the cost of building a factory complete with the necessary machinery and test equipment to produce 100,000 units per year. Apart from the design, our involvement was that we would supply training and technical support. The turnkey company had a lot of experience in delivering a licence agreement encompassing all aspects of the involvement required. If they went ahead we would receive an upfront sum of money and then a licence fee for every boiler they produced. I was told it might take some time but it was likely to happen. We had just the man for the long game: Arthur Money. Arthur and one of our young engineers, Mike Knott, went to Moscow on two occasions. They came back with a number of Russian Army watches and tales of vodka drinking parties in the back streets of Moscow but no order. The problem was how were the Russians going to pay? At the time Russia often concluded deals through a barter system. In this particular case they wanted to pay us via the supply of pig iron. Then the Berlin wall came down and Gorbachev resigned, so no licence agreement. It was an interesting experience and Arthur did get some substantial Russian watches at a very reasonable price. Arthur does come from Yorkshire; Russia was considered to be very inefficient back in the late 80s and Arthur came back with some very good tales.

In 1989 the recession was affecting a lot of industries including ours, but the growth of the combi boiler was such that by contrast we were increasing our turnover. We continued to flourish on the stock market and I began to look at ways of expanding our business abroad to capitalise on our success. I could see that we couldn't hope to sell our boilers in Europe because the market was by then overcrowded, and we hadn't been able to establish ourselves in the early days when we weren't in the Common Market. Acquisition, therefore, had to be the answer; and there was a new technology I believed would give us not only growth, but the potential once more to get ahead of the game in the UK. Condensing boilers were already entering the marketplace in both Belgium and Holland – so that was our first target and we were successful in buying the Belgian company, Radson, that manufactured them.

In a conventional boiler, the hot gases produced by burning fuel are passed through a heat exchanger, where most of their heat is transferred to water with an efficiency of just over 80%. With a condensing boiler it is possible to increase efficiency by 10-15%. The increased efficiency is achieved by the flue gases passing over a second heat exchanger. This produces condensates which creates two problems: one, how to get rid of the condensates; and two, because they are corrosive, different and more expensive materials have to be used. These difficulties mean that condensing boilers were, and indeed still are, more expensive to manufacture. Nevertheless I could see that they were going to be the future. Indeed, they are now standard in the UK.

So in 1990 we bought Radson. The management was good, and very enthusiastic. They had approximately 20% of the Belgian/Dutch market. Hank Kruithoff, the managing director, was exceptionally able and someone we had total faith in. As a result Hank joined the Group board. Nigel Collis and I travelled to Belgium every couple of months to go through the accounts and look at what progress they were making. It was a hugely successful purchase and of entirely mutual benefit.

Another opportunity to get into Europe, possibly via the back door, came about as a consequence of the Berlin Wall coming down and the unification of East and West Germany. Under Communism, the East German industry was state controlled. The new government led by Helmut Kohl set up an agency, the Treuhandanstalt, to sell off and give financial assistance to East German companies. I thought it was worth a look so I booked a flight to Berlin, having set up a meeting through the British Embassy. I took a taxi to the agency's headquarters which ironically had been the headquarters of

Hermann Göring, the Luftwaffe chief during the Second World War. It was a tall colonnaded building which stood out rather forebodingly with no other buildings in the immediate surroundings. As I mounted the 20 or so large steps to enter through a pair of massive doors, my mind went back to pictures I'd seen of Nazi Germany. Hitler, Göring, Göebbels and the other Nazi leaders must have gone up these very same steps and through the doors I was going through. It was a pretty chilling experience. I had a meeting with two or three officials of the agency and was then taken to the unimpressive East German factory which now manufactured heaters but had been an armament factory producing bullets during the Second World War. I met the management who showed me around the factory. The boilers they produced were basically gas-fired space heaters designed to be installed in the living room; grills would then be positioned in the walls and the ceiling so that heat could pass into other rooms in the dwelling. They were not very sophisticated but I assume they were fairly effective in apartments, the typical dwelling in East Germany at that time. One unusual aspect of their business was that they received just two orders a year: one for 80,000 units from the East German Government and one for 50,000 from Czechoslovakia. The factory management team and the agency staff were all very helpful. A new factory was going to be built in an industrial park nearby and the agency had been provided with substantial funds to assist foreign investment. However I came to the conclusion that it would be too risky and involve a huge commitment in time. I was also convinced it would take a very long time for a country that had been state controlled for over 40 years to accept and embrace capitalism.

Radson fitted our strategy of building one of Europe's leading heating manufacturers. Packaging Products and Metal Castings did not. They were both profitable but were businesses we did not really understand. They had been very helpful in improving our balance sheet and they also helped our group profits to a level that enabled us to go onto the London Stock Exchange.

John Cornford, knowing we would want to sell Packaging Products, approached me and asked if we would be interested in a management buy-out. In principal we had no objection providing they could raise the purchase price which they did and they have been successfully running the business ever since. John is now retired, the other two managers were bought out and John's sons (Andrew, Robert and Peter) run the company. Looking back, of course, we know that the company would not exist if we had not had an enlightened union official in Brenda Dean. She, unfortunately, was not typical. Instead, Britain's union bosses were generally old dinosaurs who believed the only good employer was a dead one. It was a tragic and misguided policy which destroyed so many British companies who simply closed up shop or moved overseas. Packaging Products is profitable and expanding however, and it's a source of great pleasure to me that John's master plan worked and his three boys are running such a successful business. Andrew, my godson, is Managing Director; Robert runs the factory and Peter is a great administrator. I and all the Cornford family were Manchester United supporters, except Peter who has loyally supported Manchester City despite having to endure Manchester United's success until 2012.

To buy Radson we needed to raise some money. I had begun to learn that the City doesn't like surprises, even good ones. It is all about growth. It doesn't matter whether you put in fantastic results, like improving your profit by 30 or 40 per cent. You would expect the share price to rise as a result, but quite often it doesn't because the City has already taken that into account. What it wants to see is that improvement repeated the following year, and the next. We invariably managed exactly that – our profit growth was above forecast - but when it came to borrowing money things were a little different. We wanted to simply make a share issue to buy Radson but unfortunately the City said the timing was not right, which was very disappointing.

Somewhat frustrated, we went to a private equity company and successfully negotiated terms. The arrangement had advantages other than purely financial; the equity company thought we should have two non-executive external directors so I asked Peter Walker, no longer in the Cabinet, to be one of them. The other was Michael Davis, already on the board of British Airways and holding a number of other directorships. Peter Walker and I went to see Michael Davis and at the end of a very good meeting Peter said to Michael: "Would you like to join us?" to which Michael said, "Do I have a choice?" It was great to have their help with our plans for the future and useful to put any plan we had to independent people and get their view from a different perspective. It added to our discipline, and if the judgments were favourable it reinforced our confidence in what we were doing.

We became something of a barometer for our particular industry and I began to find that, after talking to City analysts who contacted me to find out about the marketplace, I would read in the press that 'the City says...' and realised with some surprise that it wasn't the City – it was me.

Looking back I sometimes wish I'd used the City to expand the company via acquisitions. I believe I was establishing a rapport with the City and I was getting to know how it worked. There were several interesting companies I had targeted. Given more time, it would have been an interesting Group which I believe would have been able to survive, or would still have been attractive to Bosch. The problem with the City is that it takes the short term view. My view is that if it is to continue to be successful it has to change. The City analysts should study companies in greater depth and take into account the quality of the management, their product development, their investments and plans for the future. There should be a balanced approach. Every stock holder likes to have a fast upward moving share but most shareholders are investing for the long term. Companies should not be pressurised by the City to take a short term view at the expense of substantial growth in the long term. Shares should not be marked down because the profits might be down in the short term when the long term is looking so positive.

Long term investment should also be encouraged by the Government. Capital gains tax should be reduced to, say, 10% on shares owned for ten years. After 20 years it should be zero for people who have started their own business. That would be a fair reward because they have created employment. Their employees will have paid income tax and National Insurance. Their company will also have contributed to the local economy in many ways – paying local taxes and using local suppliers and finally will have contributed to HMRC by paying tax on its profits. Eliminating capital gains tax for successful entrepreneurs will also remove one of the advantages of moving abroad and becoming a tax exile. If successful people move abroad the Government gets nothing but if they stay they will spend their money here and more than likely be involved helping charities and the local community. Inheritance tax is another issue that needs to be looked at. There are ways of planning to transfer some wealth to your family but is 40% inheritance tax fair for an entrepreneur who has already paid income tax at 40%? I don't think so.

I remember watching that once great company, Blue Circle Cement, buckle under pressure from the City. Founded in 1900 as Associated Portland Cement by the amalgamation of 24 cement companies, it was, briefly in the 1970s, the largest cement manufacturer in the world. It had its troubles following the 1973 oil crisis but it was the pressure to diversify to maximise profits through acquisitions for companies which they knew nothing about and paid high prices for, that weakened the company. Instead of concentrating on what they did best, making cement and selling it across the world, they decided to diversify into domestic heating. They bought Potterton and another boiler company called Myson, both at hugely inflated prices. Every year they had to manipulate the figures and organise write-offs and every year they made huge losses. That's when I decided to approach them. I knew they would eventually have to sell. But I also knew I had to play a waiting game. The chairman, who had agreed to this diversification, was not going to lose face by selling out to someone like Worcester. We needed them to change their chairman.

The City eventually encouraged Blue Circle to sell their heating division, which made them vulnerable to a takeover. They even had a buyer already in waiting: the French company Lafarge, smaller than Blue Circle at the time. That way they could get the highest price. It didn't matter that Lafarge was French. It didn't matter that the head office was in France, nor did it matter that Lafarge became the world's largest cement manufacturer. Instead, what should have happened was that Blue Circle should not have been pushed into diversifying. What they should have done is build a global business in cement.

I had a vision of retiring at the age of 60, and an ambition to reach £100 million turnover. In 1994 our turnover reached £110 million. I knew then that I had to find a way of sustaining our position, to achieve the critical mass which would give the Worcester Group plc a viable future. After seeing what happened to Blue Circle and many other British companies, I didn't want to sell to a British company and see it closed down or sold off within two or three years. And I seriously believed that would have happened. It would have been crazy. Apart from letting all my employees down, it would be another loss to Britain's manufacturing base and I couldn't be a party to that. I wanted the company to go to a good home. If we sold the company, we would want it to be part of its new owner's long term strategy.

We embarked on a twin strategy. Our first choice was to continue to grow the company organically and look for strategic acquisitions. The combi was still only taking 30% of the British market and, at the time, we thought it could reach 70% or 80% (by the end of 2011 it had reached 75%).

The early 1990s were an exciting time for the company. We had built a very strong team. Our combi sales were rapidly expanding and we knew that our product range and the support we could give was outstanding. We had been the smallest UK boiler manufacturer; now we were on the way to be number one. We had a very aggressive development policy. We were now producing a high output 35 kilowatt unit which produced 50% more hot water. All our products were becoming much more sophisticated. Microprocessors were now used to make the Worcester combi more responsive and more efficient. All sorts of flue permutations were developed to increase the locations where our combis could be installed. The larger output units were now available, making our combis more attractive and so increased the sales potential of Worcester combis. Acquisitions would be a question of timing but there were a number of possibilities both in the UK and Europe. So our strategy of being able to achieve critical mass was a definite possibility.

The alternative strategy was to sell the business, but if we did, it had to be to the right company.

12

Securing The Future

I've had some good luck and some bad luck in my business life. The late 1980s and early 1990s handed me a bit of both. In 1987, the French company Saunier Duval was put up for sale. It was one of the largest boiler companies in France and had a third of the market. One of the French utility companies owned it, and I'd heard they were interested in selling. These things tend to leak; a merchant bank will ring up and say, "We hear..." because there's been a bit of chatter going on; lawyers will talk, secretaries work late and talk of a big deal in France.

I knew Saunier Duval would fit with my plan to increase critical mass by breaking into the European market. I also knew the only way to do that was to buy into it. There weren't that many possibilities. Buying in Europe is always difficult. Often the ownership is in the hands of an extended family, particularly in Germany and Italy, and often fragmented through several generations so it's extremely hard to get everyone involved to agree to sell. The younger members of the family may be willing to sell, for example, but the older members just want an annual dividend. And all European companies tend to be more nationalistic than those in Britain. Here there is a more open attitude, where everything is up for sale. It's just a question of price. Loyalty and nationality don't figure, particularly if the City of London is involved.

It was less than a year since we had gone public so it was too soon for us to be asking for a huge amount of money via the Stock Exchange to buy Saunier Duval which was many times bigger than Worcester Heat Systems. It did look good but the timing was impossible for us.

At the time, the combination boiler was selling well, although British manufacturers were on the whole pretty reluctant to acknowledge it. I wouldn't submit our figures to the Boiler and Radiator Manufacturers Association (BARMA) because I didn't want to give our competitors the information, and to some extent that prevented them from realising how well we were doing. But the merchants were aware of our success, and that was beginning to filter through so some of the leading companies did start to look at manufacturing combis. But by then we were well established. We had a very good development department. If our competitors did try to poach anyone from our team, I wasn't aware of it, and in Worcester they weren't the sort of people to sell their souls and move on. We were ahead of the game; we had a great team, our strategy was clear and we knew we always had a better product being developed in our laboratory.

Our competitors didn't realise the extent of extra support in the field that the combi boiler needed. We were using electronics for the first time on a boiler – everything was very different, both the concept and the components. Our competitors, although they had sales four or five times greater than ours at the time, had only about five or six engineers through the whole country. When they did start selling combis they hadn't got the technical or service support required and they took a lot of criticism. We made it clear that it wasn't the concept that was wrong, it was just that our competitors hadn't realised how complicated the boiler was and hadn't spent enough engineering time and effort in developing it. It wasn't an easy message to get across, but we managed it and our market share continued to rise, with the combi taking an ever increasing slice of the market. We were still bucking the trend.

At a dinner organized by BARMA at the Savoy Hotel in London, I found myself discussing the marketplace with Ian Smith of Baxi, my old friend Roy Martin from Hoval who manufactured industrial boilers, and Sinclair Thompson of Glow Worm, part of the Hepworth Group. Ian said he thought the combi boiler would make at most five or ten per cent of the market, while I was arguing against them, perhaps a little too enthusiastically, before leaving the assembled company saying, "I've no interest in selling the combi to you gentlemen, I'm off to bed.".

I often think about that conversation because about three weeks later a City journalist called me and said, "There's a British company that's bought Saunier Duval, who do you think it would be?" I said, "Well, it won't be Hepworth, Sinclair Thompson's company, because he was certainly not convinced the combi had a future when I last saw him".

Soon afterwards I heard that Hepworth had bought Saunier Duval. Sinclair Thompson had presumably been in the process of acquiring Saunier Duval when he was dismissing the combi boiler at the Savoy. My defence of it had possibly been too convincing. Maybe I should have gone to bed earlier that night.

There was another French company called e.l.m. LeBlanc, a boiler company owned by the champagne house Taittinger. Obviously boilers didn't quite fit with champagne, but the company had been extremely profitable. It then started to lose money; the management changed, there was a family tragedy, and so e.l.m. LeBlanc was very likely to be put up for sale. Unfortunately it didn't happen when I was looking for a Continental acquisition – it's always a question of timing. Tattinger put e.l.m. Leblanc up for sale in 1994 which was three years too late for my ambition to build a group that would have critical mass.

There was one other French manufacturer making combi boilers: Chaffoteaux. I knew that it had got into difficulty by going into property and had subsequently been bought by an Algerian Arab who had benefited from French government largesse. He didn't know the first thing about boilers or business and the company was continuing to make considerable losses. The banks, which are to some extent controlled by the government in France, were pressing him to sell. We flew to Paris and visited the factory a few times. Before starting negotiations we consulted our merchant bank, Lazards.

The Arab gentleman had offices just off the Champs Elysées. It was in fact a very smart flat in a beautiful position, and our negotiating team was provided with caviar and champagne. Gradually we become a little uneasy. There was no language problem, because Lazards' representative, Gerard Sander, was French but after a while I became aware that answering a question and believing we had come to a conclusion wasn't actually the case. Although they nodded and we thought they had accepted the point, later we simply returned to the same question. When I gently suggested that we might have moved on and that we had agreed, it transpired, we hadn't. "I am just accepting your position," we were told. "We must come back to that question." It was almost impossible to make progress.

In the December of that year we had a call from Lazards to say that we might have a breakthrough. Could we be at our Arab friend's country home near Paris on Christmas Eve? We thought well, why not – Chaffoteaux is number two in the French market, and if we can get the terms we want it should be OK. So Nigel Collis and I, plus Gerard from Lazards, flew to Paris and hired a taxi. The country home was in fact a large estate, rather like a small village within an immensely long brick wall, with a huge mansion at the centre. I remember there was a log fire burning as we went in – the fireplace must have been 15 feet wide with a great tree trunk on it. Once again there was smoked salmon and champagne, but as the day progressed we became increasingly aware that our Arab was not going to sign as he had promised. He had no intention of doing so. Indeed he had a Fauchon hamper ready for each of us, I assume as compensation. I should add the hampers were quite wonderful but extremely heavy and quite a problem getting through the airport, but we managed. It was some hamper!

I think our Arab friend was simply hoping that if he could hang in there and tell the bank that if companies like ours – a public company on the British stock exchange - wanted to buy Chaffoteaux, then surely it was worth further support from the bank. He did sell, eventually, to a private Italian company which could afford to take the risk and Chaffoteaux is now part of the Ariston group..

Not a lot of luck so far. I also looked at acquiring a British shower manu-facturer and a French radiator manufacturer, but neither project was successful. But during the course of my quest for a European company I made an approach to the giant German company, Bosch. Unusually for a German company, at that time they had been considering selling their heating division, but the unification of Germany in 1989 had doubled their market – and the Bonn government had gone on to encourage development of the old East Germany with subsidies for central heating. Bosch decided to keep their heating division. Then, by coincidence, during the early negotiation to buy Chaffoteaux, I had a call from Lazards. We were not alone in our quest for a purchase; Bosch were also interested. Bosch had suggested we might meet up and work together. I was interested in the idea, but as we were a public company I thought it would be difficult. After a while Bosch pulled out of the negotiations, but the acquaintance had been made. I liked what I had heard of Bosch, and the feeling, it seemed, was mutual.

Bosch was founded by Robert Bosch in 1886, when he opened a 'Workshop for Precision Mechanics and Electrical Engineering' in Stuttgart making components like electric bells and parts for telephone systems. A year later he was approached to make a magneto ignition device, based on a model made by an engine manufacturer in Cologne. Rather than just copy it, he improved on it - his guiding principle was to be continuous improvement. He was the first to adapt a magneto ignition device for a vehicle engine in

1897, and in doing so solved one of the greatest technical problems faced by the nascent automotive industry. I am sure I would have liked Robert Bosch, what he achieved was quite incredible.

Today, Bosch is a global enterprise with more than 300 subsidiaries and regional companies in over 60 countries. In 2009 its sales exceeded 38 billion euros. It employs around 270,000 people and is a leading player in the fields of automotive, industrial and building technology and consumer goods. It has an unusual ownership structure: 96% of the share capital is held by a charitable foundation with wide interests ranging from scientific research to international relations, the remaining shares being held by an industrial trust and the Bosch family. It means that in difficult times, if they have to rein back a little, they can; they don't have to pay dividends and if necessary they could renegotiate their charitable commitment – although as far as I know they've never done so. Bosch can therefore be more relaxed and take the long view rather than see only a short term future.

That has been one of this country's problems: we don't take the long view. We lack political foresight and industrial strategy. For example, in the 1950s Jaguar and Mercedes Benz were the same size, and Jaguar was technically way ahead – they were winning Le Mans, which in those days was the showcase for sports car development. Mercedes is now a world apart from Jaguar, which was bought by Tata of India in 2008, together with LandRover. Whereas Mercedes... well, you take my point. We have lost our way in so many industries. Union power was very destructive initially and now we have the City selling many of our great companies.

Now it was Bosch's turn to approach me. We were proving to be very profitable indeed. In 1991 we saw our profits increase to £5.4 million, employing about 1,000 people, increasing our market share and going exceedingly well. In 1992 Bosch asked me to visit their headquarters in Stuttgart to meet the main board directors of the group.

I couldn't help but be impressed. All the board directors spoke excellent English and were very charming; their research department was very extensive, employing hundreds of PhDs. I was particularly struck by a comment from one of the directors, when I enquired how he saw the automotive business (Bosch's main business was in the automotive field which wasn't very strong at the time). He said simply: "Extremely tough, and not very profitable, but in ten years time we will be very strong." That positive, long term attitude percolated through the whole company. I agreed with their philosophy and I could see that if we did sell Worcester Heat Systems to Bosch, then it would have a long term future prospect. It was certainly a very good alternative if my preferred option of building the company up via organic growth and acquisitions was not happening. Acquisitions, like lots of things in life, are about timing. Saunier Duval was too soon after going public; Chaffoteaux we found just impossible; e.l.m. LeBlanc would be available but it would take some time, and the unification of Germany eliminated the possibility of acquiring Junkers, the Bosch Heating Division. Blue Circle's heating division would be available, but when? I had set my retirement age at 60 and if we were to make a major acquisition I knew I would have to agree to stay for a minimum of three years. I was now 55, so had I got time? The courtship with Bosch continued for another year when a deal was put forward and I thought it looked good for our employees, good for our shareholders, and a sound basis for our future. It was put to our board, who came to the conclusion it was a very good offer. We opened negotiations in the offices of Bosch's bank, Hambros, near St James's Park in London.

It was a fine, hot summer and I often walked across the park from our flat in Mayfair to Hambros' offices during the course of what sometimes seemed endless negotiations. We shuttled back and forth between different rooms, Bosch in one room, Nigel Collis and I in another, often working very late. One fine morning I decided I wasn't going to get there for nine o'clock on the dot, and strolled across in the sunshine – no mobile phones then, of course – and was met by a very agitated chief negotiator, Clemens Börsig, who was on Bosch's main board, very concerned to know where I'd been. Normally I had not been required until 10.00am at the earliest but as luck would have it that day, I was wanted at 8.30am. Eventually we came up with a deal. Clemens and I later became very good friends and, without doubt, he is one of the brightest men I have had the pleasure of meeting.

I would have a three year 'earn-out', which meant that I would retain my own shareholding in Worcester Group and the acquisition would not be completed until the end of 1996. An earn-out means that in effect you receive your money when the earn-out date has arrived. We agreed the profit growth but risked losing if there was a downturn and things didn't go well. This works where the historical profits aren't too high but potential performance is promising, and where the individuals concerned – in this case, me – are actually a significant business asset. Our lawyers and bankers were very cautious about the idea but I was confident of what we could achieve. And I was right. We agreed that I would stay on for a period of three years with a seat on the main board of Bosch's newly formed Heating

Division. My share price would be increased by 15% each year provided we hit certain profit criteria – good if it worked, and I was prepared to take the risk. It worked.

There was one major hiccup, however. A group of shareholders opposed the deal, and in particular my own earn-out. They felt that there was an inconsistency in the fact that although I was a major shareholder I was not selling my shares, and could get that 15% growth in value each year until I retired. They had sufficient legal encouragement to make the London Stock Exchange takeover authority set up a panel to investigate the acquisition. It seemed outrageous to me. Some of those in the shareholder group had made a lot of money out of shares in Worcester Group. What hurt most, in some ways, was that one of them was an ex-colleague of mine.

I knew the investors well, and I knew, too, that they were long term investors and they would have investigated Bosch thoroughly. I remember telephoning one of them in Scotland and asking him why they were opposing the deal. They had already made a lot of money out of Worcester Group: why did they now feel they wanted more?

"Well, Cecil," he said, "we like you running the company and we want you to continue. You say we've done very well so we're very happy to continue, but if you want to sell then we think the price you've negotiated is lower than it should be. You've got a very valuable company there, and by us opposing the deal we will force someone else into the arena."

I replied: "But Bosch are a great company. I want to sell to them. I've investigated this company for a number of years now, and they are the people who will take Worcester forward. They'll be good for the employees and good for the long term future of the company."

"Cecil, with all due respect, that's not my business. My business is to do the best I can for my shareholders. If I can get a better price for my shareholders, then I'm going to do that."

It was the City at work. It didn't matter to them who bought the company. It did not matter whether it was good for our employees or good for Britain. That wasn't his business. It's how the City works. It was very disappointing.

So I went in front of the London Stock Exchange Panel on Takeovers and Mergers (the 'Panel'). An independent body, it was set up in 1968 to administer the City's code on takeovers, and to supervise and regulate takeovers. It was a bit like a court of law, with ten or twelve people there, and I suppose at the time it was a little daunting, although I felt I was right – I knew I was right. I never even contemplated being turned down, because apart from anything else, I felt that procedurally we had gone along every step in conjunction with the Panel. Had they now turned us down it would have undermined their own credibility and specifically the guy who had taken us through the procedures. Everything had been accepted by lawyers on either side. Anyway, I gave a robust defence of the deal, and pointed out that far from having a better deal than the other shareholders I was at genuine risk of losing everything. And that was true of course. Later I heard that although it hadn't been quite as straightforward as I believed, my performance was said to have carried the day.

To this day I don't know whether Bosch would have raised their offer. I was simply incensed by the fact that people who had made a lot of money were actually bringing the action at all, on what seemed to me a pretty slim pretext. Bosch was very appreciative of my stout defence of the deal – they had spent a great deal of money by then. What would have happened if the deal had not gone through? I don't know. We would probably have remained a public company. It was like a game of Monopoly, with about as much thought for the consequences for those who opposed the deal.

So, at last, the deal was done, subject to the price being agreed the following day. It was the night before the 1992 General Election.

The Labour Party, led by Neil Kinnock, was expected to win. Our German colleagues at the negotiating table, like most people, thought the stock market would consequently go down and they therefore lowered their price. I stayed up late that night. About three in the morning I realised that the Conservatives were going to get back in. The stock markets reacted very buoyantly and as a result the deal was rather better for us than for Bosch. We were very happy.

I went back to Worcester wondering how it was going to go down with the workforce. When I went into the canteen at the factory I saw that some wag had put towels over all the chairs.

13

Life With Bosch

Everyone said it would be different for me now, because I now had a boss. Well, perhaps so, but in some sense I had acquired a boss a few years earlier by becoming a public company and being answerable to outside shareholders. I had always had a sense of responsibility for my employees and I'd had to present my case at the end of each financial year. So in some ways my life didn't change. But it was challenging to be involved with the top people in the group, and of course there were the perks, like the use of the Bosch private plane – it made doing business much easier and swifter.

I was on the board of Bosch Thermotechnology, the new Heating Division, equal in status to the other three members – Gerhard Rabus, Ludwig Muller and a Mr Leidecker. It had been agreed that all board meetings would be in English, and all important documents within Bosch were in any case in German and English. On my first morning in Stuttgart when I was introduced to about 30 engineers, all of whom made a presentation on their current activity, it was announced that I too was an engineer, and the meeting would be in English – which, it seemed, everybody spoke. I had thought I might develop some linguistic expertise in German, but even the lady serving in the canteen said, "What would you like today, Mr Duckworth?" and proceeded to give me the whole menu in English. Sometimes I'd look round the boardroom and found it difficult to believe that I was the only Englishman.

Nevertheless there were differences. There was a certain formality: although Gerhard Rabus and Ludwig Muller referred to me as Cecil, and I used their Christian names, they called Mr Leidecker just that – *Herr Leidecker*. Eventually I asked why they didn't also use his Christian name. They looked at each other in mild surprise – and this was someone they had worked with for almost two years. Neither of them knew Mr Leidecker's Christian name. They promised to find out, and returned to tell me it was Hans. From that moment on I called him Hans – but they still called him *Herr Leidecker*.

They couldn't explain why. On the whole they called everyone *Herr* this or *Fraulein* that, whereas we revert to first names straight away – and of course in America you have your name on your lapel and the first thing they'll say is, "Well, whaddya think, Cecil? Good to see you".

The approach to business was different, too. A British company looks at the inflation price increases in steel or copper, for example, and expects to pass them on. A wage increase would normally be in excess of inflation. In Bosch, no increase in inflation was accepted in principle. Instead the company had to improve its manufacturing, adapt its design technique or cut overheads to meet the increase – plus saving two per cent. So, if there was an inflation increase of three or four per cent, the aim would be to save four per cent, plus two per cent – i.e. six per cent. You had to show that you were fighting inflation, not going with it and thereby adding to the problem.

Exports were given particular emphasis. The basic philosophy was that exports were essential for survival, and if you kept costs down your foreign competitors would not be able to increase their prices because they had to compete with you; it also reduced their ability to attack you in your own market. Not a strategy we're used to, although when you think about it, it is just common sense. Indeed their motto was: 'Exports count twice'.

Then there was the development of people. Bosch liked people to work in one of their international branches for a minimum of three to four years. If the language was different, you would be given assistance to learn it, and by the time you came back you would be fluent. If you didn't accept such an appointment it would almost eliminate your promotion prospects, so that was a pretty good incentive to accept an assignment in another country. Our Worcester staff were immediately able to take advantage of this, and as a result people came from Germany to Worcester and vice versa. Once again, it was a way of taking the long view, of looking to the future.

After I'd been with Bosch for several months, I had a call from the newly appointed chairman of the board of the Heating Division, Clemens Börsig. I had got to know and like Clemens during the acquisition negotiations, and when he invited me out to dinner one evening in Stuttgart he asked me what I thought about the Heating Division – was it run efficiently?

"Well," I said, "it isn't how I would run it."

"Well, how would you run it?"

"Can I have time to think about that? May I write to you?"

I wrote a list of six changes I would like to make. As a result Clemens telephoned me and said "I'm in London next week, is it possible for you to join me?" The Germans are always very polite and courteous; naturally I went to London.

I suppose I had been pretty independently minded. I was responsible for the British, Belgian and Dutch boiler markets, and of course as a board member I had a say in the management of the main Heating Division. I'd been left to get on with my particular areas without any interference, probably because things were going exceptionally well. I invited Clemens back to our flat to discuss the letter he had received from me, and he asked me about each item and put a tick against it. Then he said, "Right, that's what we'll do: but I want you to run it."

I pointed out that I lived in England and didn't speak German, but he said that didn't matter, they would provide me with a car and a flat – and asked me to stay on for a further year. I knew it would be a real challenge to run a much bigger Bosch operation but, after some thought, I said I'd do it. I became President of the Bosch Heating Division, Bosch Thermotechnology – the first non-German to head an operating division within the group. There were 15 divisions, each reporting to the main board, and it was interesting to note the culture difference; if a division wasn't doing well there was always a plan to make it profitable – not to sell it, which would have been the Anglo-American approach.

Despite reservations among certain board members, particularly my very formal colleague Hans Leidecker, I did make the changes pretty much as I had outlined. My appointment was a problem for some and I can understand those who wondered, since Bosch had bought Worcester Heat Systems, how I had ended up getting the top job... but I'm pleased to say my plan is still in place, and when I talk to my successors at Bosch they tell me it is still the blueprint. One of the members of the main board of Bosch Group told me that the Worcester acquisition was often referred to: "Remember Worcester, they had good management and we did not interfere". There is always the temptation to interfere on the basis 'we know best', forgetting that markets are different. That acknowledgement of the common sense of realising that what works in one market may not work in another, the knowledge that it has become part of the philosophy of the group is very pleasing.

Not that they always followed that route. The French boiler manufacturer e.l.m. LeBlanc which I had taken some interest in a couple of years earlier, still looked like a worthwhile acquisition with my Bosch hat on. The company was still owned by the champagne house Taittinger, so negotiating was more enjoyable than usual. Bosch decided it would be a worthwhile investment, but the family problems within the company were still somewhat tangled. The management was very poor, or non-existent. I could see this would be a major problem and pointed out that it was absolutely essential that a Frenchman should run the operation; I even said I didn't think we should go ahead unless we could find one. The French, rightly, are a very proud nation. However Bosch went ahead and asked the head of their Portuguese operation to run the LeBlanc company. He spoke quite good French but he didn't know anything about boilers, and he didn't want to live in France – he tried to commute from Portugal. It was a disaster, really. Eventually they did find a Frenchman to run it, but it took a long time for the company to be profitable.

At one point we were involved in acquiring a Chinese water heater business, and learned a similar lesson: unless you really understand another culture, probably by living in the country and knowing the language, you can make massive mistakes.

Like all big companies, Bosch had to put in place checks and balances. They have to, in case someone acts unreasonably or dishonestly. But sometimes the necessary bureaucracy was a little frustrating. When I wanted to extend the development department at Worcester, I decided not to ask permission on the basis that included in the deal was a 'clause for understanding' which allowed me certain freedom as long as it didn't involve a downward spiral in the profits. When the other board members came to Worcester and enquired "what was going on at the back there – I see you have some construction work going on?" I said, "Oh, just a small extension..." One of the board members was my former colleague Hans Leidecker, who had never been happy with my appointment as President of the board, and I have a feeling he may have reported back but I heard no more about the extension. Now the current board laugh about it, particularly as it cannot be done like that these days.

Bosch were very good to me in many ways. They never interfered with Worcester and the way I ran it. When we opened the extension to the factory at Warndon they might have expected someone from Bosch to have been invited over for the formal ceremony, but Peter Walker opened it once again.

And I did make changes. Because Bosch were great engineers, they felt they should make everything, until I pointed out that some of the components they were manufacturing were somewhat ineffective and not as advanced in technology or competitively priced because they were making them in smaller volumes. For example, they were making something like 150,000 gas valves a year whereas Honeywell were turning out 1.5 million. It took a lot of work persuading them to create a separate components division, with its own profit and loss accounts. It was a bit of a battle, but I won.

Similarly, Bosch wanted to make its own electronics and once again I said the test should be that they were competitive with an outside supplier. I said the components division must have its own accounts and stand on its own feet, not be submerged in a morass of figures so that one didn't know if it was making a loss or a profit. They accepted my view, and gradually over time we rationalized all the components. Arguments had to be justified, but if you won an argument, then they would accept it. I found the Germans were all very honorable and great to work with.

Bosch had developed some very good quality systems which I wanted to take advantage of. This has paid off; the quality of Worcester products quickly improved and are now the best in the industry. We were able to use their experience and installed a new £1,000,000 computer, vitally important in modern manufacturing, which has a fully integrated programme including financial, stock, purchasing logistics and production control. They also provided us with one of their top computer engineers for three years to fully implement the new systems. It proved to be a great marriage.

Our acquisition of Radson, the Belgian company making condensing boilers, proved very useful. Oddly enough, Germany had not developed the market in condensing boilers – nor had we – albeit we knew they would eventually be a significant part of the market. Radson's technology was transferred to Germany and England, and we now have a very comprehensive range of condensing boilers which are second to none. It was my view that the top end of the range should be manufactured in Germany, because that was their market – if you wanted an all-singing and dancing condensing boiler with knobs on that would last 20 or 30 years, then sales of that specification would be higher in Germany than Britain. Germans tend to build larger houses and put their boiler in the cellar. Buying a boiler isn't something to do light-heartedly anyway, because the cheapest boiler certainly won't be the most economical over a long period. That was why we always gave householders a choice of the whole range. And it meant the boilers in

Germany were high priced but sold in high volumes, whereas those in the middle range, made and designed here in England, tended to be good for exports elsewhere. Since then Bosch has also acquired major competitors Nefit and Buderus, both manufacturers of condensing boilers. Nefit used to be our main rival in Belgium and the Netherlands and much bigger than Radson.

I enjoyed my years with Bosch. I liked and admired the philosophy of the company and I relished the wider horizons. I made lasting friends there, too. My old negotiating partner, Clemens Börsig subsequently left Bosch for RWE, the German utility company that now owns npower here in Britain, and later joined Deutsche Bank, of which he is now chairman. We have always stayed friends. Beatrice and I recently went to his 60th birthday in Baden Baden, which was a very good long weekend.

I very much admire the German approach to industry. They believe and plan for the long term. They build the business and if it runs into difficulties, they don't put it up for sale, they fix it. They invest in research and they invest in people. When I first visited Bosch we were still pursuing our strategy of building the company up so that it had critical mass and would therefore be able to be sustainable. After my first visit, having been taken around their Research and Development Department and aware of the commitment to the long term, I had already taken the view that Bosch would be a very good alternative.

I finally retired at the end of 1996, selling my 30% share very satisfactorily, but also taking huge pleasure in the fact that I had done what I had set out to do – secure the future of the factory, the research and development department and the workforce I had seen grow from the days when it was just me in the Old Vinegar Works. I was presented with two bronze busts of myself, one of which is displayed at Worcester and the other at the Clay Cross factory. Today Worcester Bosch is planning to expand even further but it will, I hope, remain in the city; and I hope Worcester will always value it. Bosch has been very good for Worcester and the UK economy. In the first place there was an inward investment of almost £100,000,000. It was good for our employees: the company now employs over 1,700 people. It has also been a very good acquisition for Bosch as well as for all the shareholders, including myself. After I sold my shares, I was listed alongside Nick Faldo in the *Sunday Times* Rich List. I just wondered at the time if any of his golfing ability might rub off on me! It hasn't yet, but I remain hopeful.

As for what I was going to do in retirement...Well, a couple of years before I had been approached by Worcester Rugby Club to see if I could help them with a lottery bid. I said I'd think about it. It might be a bit of fun. Perhaps I'd come and have a look at the project... And that was just the start.

14

Rugby

Richard Burton once said, "Rugby is a wonderful show: dance, opera and, suddenly, the blood of a killing." Is that part of the attraction? Joy, and then a violent end? Maybe. I have spent countless hours watching 15 – often fewer - men trying to get an oval ball from one end of a field to the other by evading or essentially attacking another 15. Just occasionally I have watched as one of them swooped to the turf or sent the ball singing between those high white posts, and heard the crowd erupt in ecstasy. I have felt exultation and hope – but also, and too often, frustration and despair.

Yet P. G. Wodehouse also wrote: "Rugby football is a game I can't claim absolutely to understand in all its niceties, if you know what I mean. I can follow the broad, general principles, of course. I mean to say, I know that the main scheme is to work the ball down the field somehow and deposit it over the line at the other end and that, in order to squelch this programme, each side is allowed to put in a certain amount of assault and battery and do things to its fellow man which, if done elsewhere, would result in 14 days without the option, coupled with some strong remarks from the Bench."

It is, undoubtedly, an extraordinary game. Said to have been invented at Rugby school when a boy named William Webb Ellis 'with a fine disregard for the rules of football as played in his time, first took the ball in his arms and ran with it' in 1823. Rugby didn't even have any written rules until 1845. Indeed, the laws of the game have always been in a state of change, and the process hasn't stopped today. Rugby union was born out of the schism in 1895 that led to the creation of rugby league, and in 1900 it was introduced into the Olympic Games in Paris. France, then Germany and Great Britain all entered teams – and France won gold.

I had played very little rugby, being too light, but I had developed a very keen interest in the game during my trips from Worcester back to Macclesfield where my old school friend Peter Holland had become a very good scrum half. Macclesfield is a very fine club, they had an excellent side and played exciting running rugby back in the late 1950s. Peter went on to play for Cheshire and the Northern Counties which was then a stepping stone to the full England squad but Macclesfield unfortunately was not considered to be a fashionable club so he didn't quite make it and play for England. When I arrived in Worcester in the 1960s, Beatrice introduced me to her local club.

Worcester Rugby Football Club owes its origin to the Reverend Francis Eld, headmaster of Worcester Royal Grammar School on whose Flag Meadow ground the team first turned out in blue knickerbockers and white shirts bearing the city's coat of arms in November 1871. There were a good many disbandings and revivals after that first match against the Worcester Artillery – which Worcester Rugby Football Club won easily – but by the 1960s the club was well established. They had a ground and clubhouse at Bevere and despite some financial problems (so what's new) they were playing five sides; in 1966/67 the 1st XV had the best season in the club's history, and the Wanderers, then the third and fourth teams, were likewise smashing records.

Beatrice knew many of the members and players, and we became regular supporters, building up lifetime friendships with people like Jeremy Richardson, Bernard Blower, Derek Thompson, Don Everton and Brian Wilkes. In 1975 the club moved to Sixways, soon to be floodlit, and in 1980 Worcester Rugby Club went on tour to the USA and Canada. It flourished through the 1980s and in 1992 the then President, local solicitor and very good friend of mine, David Hallmark, in consultation with the North Midlands RFU, first put forward Worcester's suitability as a centre of excellence for youth rugby.

I was then president of Bosch heating division, and didn't have a lot of spare time, but when David approached me to help with the club's ambitious project, I agreed to look at it. They wanted to apply to the Sports Council and Sport England for money to create an indoor training centre, a new pitch and stand, but it required money, which they did not have, to make a bid. The application had to be professionally presented, involved quantity surveyors, architects and others, so I knew it was going to be costly. I was invited to Sixways to see the plans and watch a game of rugby; it was a bright sunny day, and plans for the project were set out on an easel. There were about 50 people there. I thought the plan was pretty impressive, but primitive – at that stage they were just putting rough ideas on paper so I told them I would go away and think about it. I was interested: retirement was just three years away and I felt this could be something to take on.

The biggest club in the West Midlands at the time was Moseley, although in decline. They were certainly not the club they once were. Nevertheless they hadn't then lost their ground – that came later, in 1998 – and Worcester was still a sort of feeder club for them. If any young players came through, the natural progression was to go to Moseley. Worcester had a very good young player called Carl Arntzen who had played for England in the Under 21s and wanted to play at Moseley to progress his rugby career. Don Everton asked if I would take him on to do a sandwich degree at Wolverhampton in engineering. He spent six months with Worcester Heat Systems and six months at university which proved to be very successful. Carl continued to play for Moseley and after receiving his engineering degree he joined Worcester Heat Systems. At the time, Moseley was one of the top clubs in the country and if you wanted to play for England you had to play for a top club. A player with a smaller club really couldn't progress because they couldn't get the fixtures with the top clubs. It was, in truth, a system designed to make sure that the fashionable clubs would remain fashionable, and they weren't letting go of their fixture list - a situation that prevailed until the leagues were introduced in 1987.

It was undoubtedly a huge challenge to turn Worcester into a centre of rugby excellence. The maximum contribution from Sport England was two thirds of the total cost of the project, and we had to guarantee that we could raise the other one third of the cost. Then there was the cost of the application so it would have to be a huge commitment.

Having seen the rough plan that the club had in mind, I went away to consider whether I should back the bid and become involved. The three questions I asked myself were: (1) Was it possible to get Worcester into the top flight of English rugby, given it would take five or six promotions to get them from the Midlands One division where they were at the time? This was 1992 and there was talk of the game going professional although it was amateur at the time (the game went professional in 1995). (2) Could I turn Worcester into a Rugby city like Gloucester and Bath? Worcester was a similar size and, like Gloucester and Bath, didn't have a successful football team. At the time both Bath and Gloucester rugby clubs were attracting crowds of about 5,000; on a good day, Worcester only had about 100 supporters when the sun was shining. And (3) Could I repeat my industrial success and do it again in rugby?

There were several things going for Worcester Rugby Club. It was located on the edge of the city, only 600 yards from Junction 6 on the M5.

Worcestershire had never had a successful winter sports team. Worcester City had a population of 100,000 but the county had a total of 500,000 and Birmingham was only a short drive away. Taking all these factors into account, I thought that I would like to have a go.

I went back to David Hallmark and his fellow members and said I was interested in helping with the Lottery bid, and that if we were successful I would contribute one third of the cost, provided the club raised £50,000, as I thought that they should make a contribution. There were, I remember, a number of people who almost fell off their chairs when I said I wanted to take Worcester into the Premiership. I also said that I would form a separate company, Worcester Rugby Trading Limited. I wasn't very good with committees, and I wanted complete responsibility for the development of the club and its commercial operations. There was a certain silence at that point. I said that if they didn't want me, I would understand and there would be no hard feelings; I wanted the club's support to be unanimous for my proposals. As far as I know there were no dissenters. Indeed, there was much excitement and enthusiasm.

So we went ahead. Architects and surveyors were briefed and set to work. I decided to make the design a little more futuristic – for instance, the wavy top to the stand – just to make it a bit more attractive and eye-catching to those looking at the application. It cost about £60,000 just to prepare the bid, but we were successful, and by 1996 we had close on £2 million with which to build the new stand, clubhouse, roads and floodlighting. The Lottery provided £1,300,000 and I made up the balance. Unfortunately the club didn't raise the £50,000 it had promised; it seems that when someone comes along who is wealthy, people tend to feel they don't really need to do any more. It's unfortunate and it's something I found disappointing, and still do. I have found some members of the amateur club very difficult - whatever we do for them, they always want more. The vast majority, however, are very pleased with the progress of the Club. Whatever you do in life however, there are always a few short-sighted malcontents.

Otherwise we were off to a good start, and although I was still working at arm's length from the project, I was in touch with everything that was going on, which was a good deal at that time. Work went ahead on the new facilities and in the meantime we were playing on one of the side pitches. Worcester Rugby Club was then in Midlands One division and our coach was Phil Maynard. Phil was very good at identifying players in other clubs and getting them to come to Worcester. In those days, while the game was still amateur, we were allowed to give the players travelling expenses – all based on mileage and agreed by the RFU. I noticed if five people were coming from Birmingham in one car, they all claimed expenses as individuals – which I chose to ignore. Oddly enough we were helped by a rift at Moseley where the coach was proving to be a little dictatorial and upsetting a number of their best players; we benefited substantially as several of their players, including their captain, Peter Shillingford joined Worcester. Peter was a very good player and an excellent captain and his move to Worcester proved to be a catalyst. Neil Lyman and Mark Linnett followed, both exceptional front row men. Worcester was then the club others wanted to join. Bruce Fenley and Chris Raymond came from Gloucester and Steve Lloyd, a giant of a man, joined us from Harlequins. Nick Baxter then arrived and became a favourite with Worcester supporters. Nick was a prolific try scorer and still holds the record of 151 league tries. I have great memories of him running down the wing and scoring; on one occasion he did a cartwheel as he scored - the game was on TV and the commentator said that was not to be recommended. Of course, he could have dropped the ball, but Nick was a showman and the crowd loved him. And we won the Midlands One division at our first attempt without losing a game.

But rugby was about to undergo fundamental change. In 1995 the International Rugby Board (IRB), governing body of the game, made a somewhat unexpected announcement after meeting in Paris. They had decided to make rugby union professional. Rugby, it declared, was now an 'open game'. Turning professional was seen as the only way of ending the hypocrisy of 'shamateurism' and preventing players leaving for rugby league, which was already professional and paying large salaries, particularly in Australia. Here, too, there had been some blurring of the definition of amateur. Bath, for instance, had arranged for many of their players to have jobs which allowed them a good deal of free time to train. Don Everton, who had captained Worcester in the 1950s had brought players from abroad to Worcester, putting them up rent free to give them experience of living in England. One of them was Ruben Kruger who later developed into a magnificent player for South Africa and was one of their key players when they won the World Cup in 1995.

In Newcastle the owner of Newcastle United, Sir John Hall, - "not a rugby man" as he said of himself - was swift to pre-empt the RFU in England. He already had a vision of creating a sporting club, encompassing rugby union as well as football and other sports, and he wasted no time in buying Newcastle Gosforth Rugby Club. He immediately recruited Wasps and

England fly-half Rob Andrew as captain and star player, as well as a raft of other high-profile signings. The team acquired a new name, Newcastle Falcons; changed its home colours to black and white and went on to rise through the second tier of English club rugby to clinch promotion to the Premiership and then become league champions.

To some extent it was an inevitable change, and although Sir John Hall rather jumped the gun, the phenomenon of 'shamateurism' had long been acknowledged. It wasn't exactly a modern practice: I believe members of an Australian club touring Britain in 1908 had been paid 21 shillings a week. And in the 1990s many players were employed by people who were very generous with their time, shall we say... Bath was one of the most successful clubs at using this technique, and became one of the top clubs in Europe as a result. It had built up a huge following at its lovely but rather archaic ground, called the 'Rec'.

I knew that we too would have to go professional, and we were one of the first clubs at the lower end of the market, as it were, to do so. So we started to employ a full time coach and pay our players. Rugby players weren't highly paid in those days, but the cumulative total cost was quite high, so expenditure began to be close on £1 million a year. Our income in no way covered that so we were making huge losses, but as we began to accelerate our progress to the top, we were getting bigger crowds. When we played London Welsh we got a crowd of over 4,000 and I remember thinking we were well on the way to the breakeven figure of 6,000.

Going professional also meant that our coach, Phil Maynard, would have to embrace the change to a seven days a week commitment. Could he do it? I felt we had to look ahead and contacted Jon Callard, who was just coming to the end of his international career – he had won five caps for England and wanted to get into coaching. He played for Bath and was a very good kicker, a key factor in rugby. We had agreed terms when suddenly Bath decided they wanted a fee for letting him go. We settled on £15,000, quite a lot of money at that time, but Jon said, "Don't pay it. I've done a lot for this club and they ought to give me a free transfer".

While these discussions were going on I was invited to the launch of the new facilities at Twickenham, having just bought a box in the new west stand. At the lunch I found myself sitting next to Les Cusworth, legendary fly-half for Wakefield, Leicester Tigers and England. Les had run the England Under 21 and the England Sevens team, and was now assistant to Jack Rowell, the England head coach. He was pretty suspicious of professionalism and didn't really believe it was going to work, but he gave me his card and asked me to contact him if he could help us in the future. I was still trying to negotiate with Bath but I was beginning to wonder if we would ever make any progress. Finally I decided to telephone Les. We met, and I decided to choose Les for our new coach instead of Jon. Looking back on it now, I wonder how different life might have been if I had chosen Jon Callard.

But the deed was done and Les Cusworth brought a lot to Worcester. He is an interesting person; but not, in my view, a good man-manager. It's not easy to handle a bunch of players when you are only playing 15, with seven on the bench. Some are bound to be unhappy and it's a difficult situation to manage. Nevertheless we won promotion and reached what was then called National Division One – now called the Championship, the league below the Premiership.

We were on our way.

15

Whistleblower

The world of professional rugby was, and to some extent still is, a jungle. Had the transition from the amateur game been orchestrated over a period of time, and notice been given that it was to happen over, say, three years, the change to a professional game would perhaps have worked better. But in those early days, clubs like Richmond and London Scottish simply went bust and others, like Moseley, had to sell their grounds. Some clubs did spend their money wisely. Initially there were two leagues each consisting of 14 clubs. There was a system of two up, two down - relegations and playoffs. Clubs at the top in the Courage League (equivalent to the Premiership today) wanted to reduce the number of clubs being promoted and relegated, whereas those at the bottom wanted more. So of course there was conflict.

There was, and still is, tension between the RFU, which is responsible for the rules and governance of the game, and Premier Rugby Limited (PRL) which is now composed of the twelve clubs competing in the top league. Nevertheless in 2001 they got together to create another organisation, the England Rugby Board, specifically to manage the elite professional game in England.

As for Worcester: well, we gained promotion each year and by the 1999/2000 season we were in National Division One and battling to gain promotion to the promised land of the Premiership but we were just edged out by long term rivals Leeds. For three years we were known as the bridesmaids of Division One, each time coming second to Leeds or Rotherham.

One of the prime movers behind the PRL was Tom Walkinshaw of Gloucester Rugby Club. He was already a legendary figure, a formidable operator in motorsport and Formula 1, when he bought Gloucester in 1997. He and Charles Jillings of Harlequins took the view that it would be quite nice to pull up the drawbridge and have no promotions or relegations. They drew up entry criteria for getting into the Premiership which precluded almost anyone from being able to fulfill them. For example, clubs seeking promotion couldn't have a ground capacity smaller than any of the current members of the Premiership. That was 7,000 at Sale Rugby Club. They also said that new clubs like Worcester couldn't play at a football ground, whereas many rugby clubs did – including Premiership clubs Saracens, London Irish and London Wasps. But although they were allowed to break the rule, apparently newcomers weren't. And then there was the money. Money apportioned from the centre to the clubs was significantly less to a newly promoted club compared to that distributed to the existing members of the Premiership. A period of eight years had to elapse before parity was achieved. These new conditions were an attempt to ring fence the Premiership by stealth.

So there were a lot of barriers. First, we had to have the capacity – and why should we have capacity for 7,000 when we normally got only 5,000 maximum? We couldn't escape that rule by playing at a football ground. Then, if we did manage to get into the Premiership, we were disadvantaged financially because we had 40% less income than the clubs we were competing with. It was pretty difficult, and in my view, unjust and very unfair.

Indeed, so widespread was the belief that the twelve Premiership clubs were conspiring to keep themselves as an exclusive elite that an official investigation was carried out by the Office of Fair Trading in 2002. First Division Rugby (FDR – representing the 14 clubs in National Division One) alleged that the requirements set down by PRL for entry into the Premiership would deny promotion to some of their members. The OFT upheld the concerns and PRL was obliged to revise its entry criteria to allow more flexibility.

Everybody involved at the top of the game at that time, including the RFU, believed that there would always be promotion and relegation; it was like oxygen, it was the air that we breathed. It was the mood of the nation. There was later to be a decisive meeting between the RFU and Premiership Rugby which ensured that promotion and relegation would remain a feature of domestic club rugby in England at least until 2016. That came as a blow to the PRL. There was talk of deception by the RFU, but the RFU declared they had never made any commitment to end the system and they had acted in the belief that to maintain the system was what the grass roots of rugby had decided.

At the time I was Chairman of National Division One and a member of the RFU Council; as Will Carling (former Captain of England) put it: "One of the 57 old farts". I went to the Council meeting purely out of interest to see how the RFU operated and I have to say they were not all 'old farts'. Most council members put in a tremendous amount of time in promoting and running amateur rugby in England. The problem was that once the game had gone professional the structure was inappropriate. Most Council members had jobs or they were retired so they were only part-time and therefore did not have the time or the ability to run what now had become a significant operation. The Council recognised this and employed a team of professional people: a managing director, financial director, marketing director, etc. to run the operation. But unfortunately the Council members could not resist interfering. They did not seem to accept that their role was to run amateur rugby and let the executive run Twickenham and the professional game. They should have acted like non-executive directors in a public company, holding the executive to account but allowing them to manage; if, of course, the executive did not deliver then they could vote for a change.

In the 2000/2001 season we ended up coming second yet again. We lost games we should have won against Moseley and Coventry - both teams we would have beaten nine out of ten times but on an off day you can lose, particularly in a local derby. Leeds was promoted to the Premiership and Rotherham relegated to join us in National Division One.

One afternoon I took a call from Tom Walkinshaw.

"Cecil," he said cheerfully, "do you want to be in the Premiership?"

I said yes, of course, that was after all our *aim*.

"Do you want to be in it this year?"

I asked what he meant, and he said, "Well, we're having trouble with Leeds. They won't accept the terms. If you were asked to join us, would you do so?"

I pointed out that we hadn't prepared for the Premiership, but I suppose we'd have a go – which in retrospect was the wrong thing to say. I should have said no, it was our ambition but we didn't want to get in by default – and I probably didn't help Leeds' cause. In the end, Leeds had to accept the terms of entry into the Premiership. Tom Walkinshaw and others set about trying to further eliminate promotion and relegation. That, of course, was the object: to eliminate promotion and relegation by stealth. We had a lot

Signing the Bosch deal with Clemens Borsig

The Worcester Bosch headquarters in Worcester

With Beatrice aboard the Orient Express in 1992 en route to Venice

(Left to right) Rod Haynes, Managing Director of Stelrad; Reg Wade, Managing Director, Grundfos; myself and John Footman, Chairman, Plumb Centre, and Director of Wolseley-Hughes

At Buckingham Palace after receiving the OBE in 2004

CITY OF WORCESTER

In pursuance of a resolution passed at a special meeting of the City Council on the twenty ninth day of July 2008

IT WAS RESOLVED

that in recognition of the contribution he has made to the business, sporting and educational life of the City and through the Duckworth Worcestershire Trust his contribution to the City's environment and landscape

CECIL DUCKWORTH
OBE DL CEng

BE ADMITTED AS AN Honorary Freeman of the City of Worcester

The Common Seal of Worcester City Council was affixed in the presence of:

Mayor

The citation presented to me by the Mayor of Worcester on my admission as a Freeman of the City in 2008

Winning the Championship Trophy in 2011

Mark, Beatrice, Jill and I at Buckingham Palace 2004

The new East stand at Sixways

(L-R) Nigel Collis, Arthur Money, me, Roger Tomlinson and Kevin Lee

Miles Benjamin and Matt Mullen in action against Sale at Sixways
2009/2010

Pat Sanderson and Craig Gillies against Gloucester at Sixways 2010

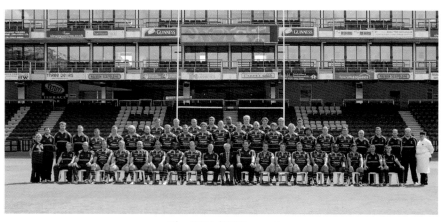

The 2011/2012 squad

of meetings about this subject with Tom and we were often summoned to various places such as Tom's office in Oxfordshire, London or Manchester at fairly short notice, and we would troop along to discuss promotion and relegation. But of course we never made any progress whatsoever. It was as if Tom was always orchestrating these meetings to ensure that we would, in the end, back off.

I think that Tom thought the emergence of Worcester would be detrimental to Gloucester, which was why he took a particular interest in our success. I had dinner with him on a number of occasions in Cheltenham when he tried to persuade me that Worcester could be a satellite club of Gloucester. I pointed out that having come so far, we weren't going to back off now; I'd made a commitment to take Worcester into the Premiership and that was what I was intending to do. I told him that although we didn't agree with the rules of entry to the Premiership, we would abide by them. We certainly didn't believe we should be disadvantaged financially in the first eight years, but our appetite for success was not diminished one jot.

The following season, 2001/2002, we were once more in a fierce battle with Rotherham. They were a good side and had the advantage of a difficult ground at Clifton Lane. We were winning most games pretty easily and Rotherham were skilled at rotating their players, resting them so that they could come to the boil for the matches with us. Yet again we were the bridesmaids, while Rotherham was now able to be promoted to the Premiership and this time, Leeds was relegated. For Leeds it would mean a so-called 'parachute payment' of some £720,000, designed to ease the pain of relegation, and for Rotherham - despite its lack of facilities – a chance to establish themselves among the rugby elite.

But Rotherham didn't get promoted. And Leeds didn't get relegated. We were told later that a payment of £600,000 was to be given to Rotherham as compensation. Suddenly the politics of the Premiership, if true, looked murky.

First, there was rumour: talk that there had been an agreement between the Premiership and Rotherham, that if Rotherham won the league they wouldn't accept promotion. I didn't know about any such agreement. Then I had a call from a journalist to say there was indeed an agreement, and a letter accompanying it from Tom Walkinshaw to Mike Yarlett, Chairman – the financier – of Rotherham. I said, "Well, find a copy of this letter". It did not appear. But in the summer of 2002 I was telephoned by the same journalist who told me he had just interviewed Keith Barwell, Chairman of Northampton Rugby Club, who had admitted that there was an agreement by Premier Rugby that if Rotherham finished top of the league, they wouldn't accept promotion. I asked the journalist if he would mind if I telephoned Keith Barwell. He said no, he had no objection, so I did.

I spoke to Keith twice. He said, "Well, Tom is a great negotiator. He told us he could solve this promotion and relegation issue, but it would cost us £50,000 each". That meant that each Premiership club would pay £50,000 into the pot and that money would go to Rotherham, who of course would then be able to get new players among other things, and so have a good chance of beating Worcester. That couldn't be guaranteed, but £600,000 would do a lot to prevent us becoming champions and would, effectively, keep us out of the Premiership.

Then, in August 2002, I received a letter signed simply 'A Friend'; no name. And it said: 'I suggest you ask Jillings, Walkinshaw and Yarlett about a meeting on 16 August 2002 in Investec Bank, Broad Street, St Helier'. Charles Jillings was the chairman of Harlequins; Tom Walkinshaw of Gloucester Rugby Club, and Mike Yarlett of Rotherham. We telephoned the Investec Bank in Jersey to check if there had been such a meeting. And sure enough, there had. We were told by the bank staff that in their diary was recorded 'PRL meeting 11am'. But no names. The odd thing was, when we checked again with the Investec Bank, they couldn't find the diary that had all the meeting dates in the bank. It had disappeared.

I don't know who wrote that letter. Whoever it was evidently didn't like Messrs Jillings, Walkinshaw and Yarlett, or maybe had a vendetta against them. But what was disappointing was that they were not prepared to put their name to it. They had got my home address from somewhere; the only clue to their identity was a postmark on the envelope: SW8 5BB.

I reported the matter to the RFU. Meanwhile the *Daily Telegraph* broke a story about a special slush fund that had been set up to bribe Rotherham into failing to meet the criteria for being promoted to the Premiership. The official reason for failing to get promotion was that they had 'failed to provide the required documentation relating to ground-sharing with Rotherham United Football Club'. I met RFU officials at Twickenham: Chief Executive Francis Baron, Chairman Graeme Cattermole and Disciplinary Officer Robert Horner were given the job of pursuing an investigation into the alleged scandal. In December the RFU announced that an independent inquiry was to be set up, headed by a leading barrister, Anthony Arlidge QC.

The Premiership realised they might be in
about a so-called slush fund were true, si
to all the rules and certainly couldn't be
closed ranks. They took on a top barrister
the PRL clubs would attend a meeting with
did say was that Barwell had apparently saic
warnings had nipped the plot in the bud, anc
to anyone.

It was now the be
Otley. We had t
minutes to
In the
won

The Arlidge report couldn't get anywhere, o
interviewed except for Rotherham's owner, Mi   ...uge noted that
'cooperation from Premier Rugby has been most disappointing and that has
made my task more difficult'. Of Rotherham he said: "They demonstrate
both an initial casualness of approach and a willingness to manipulate facts
to fit a required situation... the forensic accounting exercise has failed to
unearth any evidence to indicate that anything improper went into the
accounts of Mr Yarlett's companies or family. The cynical would say that
they wouldn't find it, would they?" He nevertheless concluded there was
insufficient evidence that any payment was in fact made, and some positive
evidence suggesting that none was.

In retrospect I realise that the RFU and Anthony Arlidge were powerless to
pursue the matter further. I think some of the clubs just took things too
far. Keith Barwell, being a very honest and genuine man, realised that the
proposal was ridiculous and warned they would get found out. In the end,
the clubs were fined although I don't think they ever paid up. I'm sure
Anthony Arlidge and the RFU knew that there had been some skullduggery
going on in an attempt to prevent Worcester being promoted. But the reality
was that it could not be proved so the whole sorry episode was swept under
the carpet.

What was astonishing to me was that if the PRL were going to financially
assist Rotherham to not accept promotion, did they think we would just
give up and walk away? If they did, they don't know me. We would simply
try again, again and again until we were successful.

The end result was that Leeds, having finished bottom of the Premiership,
did not get relegated. I cannot be certain of course that any money was paid
to Rotherham but if not, there is a lot of evidence to suggest that there was
an intention to do so. I concluded one thing was for certain, it would not
happen again.

ginning of the new season. Our first game was away to
wo players sent off and were losing by seven points with five
go. Otley had a very good front row. Then we scored a penalty.
st two minutes of play we scored a try right under the posts and
It was the start of something. In that season, 2003/2004, we won every
game we played: 26 out of 26. We were finally promoted to the Premiership.
We had achieved our first ambition; the question was - could we stay there?

16

In The Scrum

Looking back over the past few years, I can relive a number of moments, good and bad, that mark my life with Worcester Rugby Club. The Warriors had won promotion to the Premiership. Sixways has grown from strength to strength, and is still expanding. But rugby isn't quite like industry. I can handle factory fires, global oil crises and boiler breakdowns, but the RFU is a different matter. And I soon learned that there is only one way to go from the top, and that's down. Almost as soon as we reached the sunny uplands of the Premiership, we became the favourites to be relegated. We were about to have six years of excitement, a lot of heart-stopping moments and some frustration and disappointments thrown in. Even as we began to plan for the future, the rug was very nearly pulled from under us.

By the end of February 2004 we knew we would almost certainly win the National Division One league. The minimum standards for entry into the Premiership had been raised to require that a club's ground should now have a capacity of at least 10,000, but we had plans to expand our stadium to meet the criteria. In the meantime we had applied to our district council, Wychavon, for the necessary planning permission to build a temporary stand. There was only one objection: from Rotherham. Apparently we had made some minor error in filling in the forms. It seems one doesn't have to have a local interest - even someone living in Beijing can object. We have some very strange planning rules in this country.

You might say Rotherham is a long way from Worcester. You might also say it was against the spirit of everything you think of as fair play, here in England in the 21st century where you would think there is still a degree of decency. If our planning application had gone to judicial review, it probably would have resulted in dismissal of the objection by the presiding judge. But the fact they objected was disgraceful.

Fortunately the RFU took a pragmatic view and said that even if we hadn't crossed every 't' and dotted every 'i', our intention was clear. The PRL knew Rotherham's objection was based on pretty flimsy grounds and would not go down too well with the public. To have gone to judicial review would have created a huge financial problem. Although the RFU and the PRL eventually said our promotion should go ahead, the hiatus created real anxiety for our players, for our supporters and for the new players who had signed for us. Sadly, however, there were some people who wanted us kept out of the Premiership at all costs.

So, at last, we were in the Premiership. I remember sitting round the table with my fellow PRL chairmen, people I knew pretty well. Most were reasonable. I said, "I'll put you on notice that I disagree with the way a club that is promoted to the Premiership is funded. I don't agree that we should have to wait eight years for equal funding".

The response was: "Look, you've just come into the Premiership, but we've spent a lot of money establishing it. Why should you come in and get an equal share?"

My reply was that I'd spent a lot of money too, but they didn't think that was a legitimate reason for me having an equal share. The eight years, they said, would prevail. In fact, after five years I pointed out that I had met all the criteria for entry and a lot of clubs around that table had not. Wasn't it about time this was looked at again?

Eventually they did agree with me, and this time reason prevailed. But even then some complained that they were going to lose £100,000 per club. To them, it wasn't a question of what was fair, it was all about the money. It irked me then and it still does. But that was the environment I was in, and if I was going to live in it then there was no point in inviting hostility. I kept my thoughts to myself.

However, we had to be on our mettle. I knew that. We had to attract top players and we had to develop young players. The Worcester Warriors Academy was one of the first to be created and well before the RFU's new regional academy programme was introduced in 2002, and we now have a strong history of developing home grown talent. There's no greater pride than in seeing one of our very own Academy players pull on a first team jersey. We've already seen the benefits of our Academy programme in the last few seasons, with several top class players now regulars in both our first team and international squads. And it isn't just about finding the stars of the future. It's also about producing talented, educated and well-rounded young men. I had wanted and believed that we should have a strong academy similar in a way to the strong development department I had had in my industrial life.

The Academy also made us vulnerable. Not long after it came into being, Gloucester decided to follow our example – and recruited our Academy manager. Clubs began to recognise our ability to produce talented young players. They were like vultures, sitting in the trees waiting for the opportunity to pick off our home-grown talent. And of course they would tell them they are more likely to get into the England squad if they go to a more established club, because they'll be playing with players already in the England side. Where would you rather go, clubs would ask them: a club with some history at the top of the Premiership or someone hovering around the bottom?

For Worcester Warriors it meant not only was everyone trying to poach our talent, but our ability to attract good players was also reduced. If players did come, we had to pay a premium for them, so we were in danger of losing the strength in depth we needed because we couldn't afford sufficient players – assuming, that is, we kept within the wage cap. There have been some creative ways of circumventing the wage cap set by the Premiership clubs, and there are some suspicions that it is still happening. Currently it is £4,500,000; the total amount any single club can spend on its playing squad.

Having reached the Premiership, we were optimistic and hopeful. Our first game was against Newcastle Falcons and Jonny Wilkinson at Sixways and it was on TV. It was a glorious sunny day and there was a lot of optimism but we lost 9-30. Jonny Wilkinson signed autographs as soon as he came off the pitch and continued for two hours until the Newcastle team bus left.

Much was going to depend on how we organized ourselves. Our Director of Rugby during our battle to get into the Premiership and for the first three years as a Premiership club was John Brain, a quiet West Country man and law graduate with no taste for publicity. We shared some tense times, notably a dramatic end of season day in April 2005 when we played Northampton at home. There were five teams on that final day facing relegation: Harlequins, Leeds, London Irish, Northampton and ourselves.

Harlequins had had a grim season and were favourites to go down, but we were pretty much defying the odds by surviving. We knew that we had to win against Northampton Saints. Northampton knew that if they lost, then Sale Sharks would have to beat Harlequins to prevent the Saints being relegated. We were losing until the last seven or eight minutes of the match, when we had worked the ball into Northampton's 22. Tony Windo suddenly did a reverse pass to Drew Hickey who was coming in at speed at a great angle and crashed over the line. Sixways erupted. That moment will live with me forever. It was tense enough at Sixways that afternoon, with a capacity crowd of 10,000 including Keith Barwell, Northampton's chairman, but the Northampton supporters also had their eyes on the match and ears on their radios to hear what was happening at the Stoop. Then Sale scored a try: they were winning. Suddenly, in the 80th minute, there was a penalty for Harlequins. You could hear the hush among Northampton supporters all around Sixways. The ball drifted wide of the left post. Harlequins had lost to Sale Sharks, 22 to 23. If the penalty had been converted Harlequins would have survived and Northampton would have been relegated. We had won 21 to 16, Northampton were safe and Harlequins were relegated.

There were great celebrations at Sixways among the Worcester and Northampton supporters and a lasting bond was formed between the two clubs, albeit one that was severely tested during the following season when we were both back in the relegation area. On the final Saturday, 28 April 2006, Northampton Saints were playing London Irish at home and we were up against Saracens at Sixways. We were just one point in front of Northampton. If we won – and we had more wins than Northampton - we would survive; but if we lost and Northampton won, then we would go down. We tore into Saracens and beat them convincingly (22-7) and although Northampton won their game, it didn't matter to us. We survived, and Northampton Saints were relegated. Just another heart stopping game...

The strain was beginning to tell. I had begun to feel that although John Brain had done a good job for us, we couldn't afford to go on rattling around at the bottom of the league. John was keen to get on and develop the club, and we had just signed several big name players including the All Black, Rico Gear, who had a fantastic record for scoring tries. But I felt we needed someone now with a proven track record, both at club and international level, to take the team forward. I'd heard that Mike Ruddock, who had won the Grand Slam for Wales in 2005, was available. The circumstances of his departure from Wales were somewhat mysterious, but I took the opportunity to talk to him about his – and our – future. He said he would like to take us on. I then had the very difficult job of telling John Brain the following Monday morning that he was no longer required. It was very uncomfortable for both of us. It had been a difficult decision as John had worked so hard and his wife and family had been so supportive. He had achieved a lot for Worcester. But it's a cruel world. Winning isn't easy.

His replacement, Mike Ruddock, had had an interesting career. He had broken his leg when he was on the edge of gaining a cap for Wales. Unfortunately the break finished his playing career so he moved on to coaching. He had a lot of success at club level and, as a result, was appointed Head Coach for Wales. It was an enlightened appointment; Wales won the Grand Slam for the first time since 1978, playing a great off-load and attacking game which we hoped Mike would bring to Worcester. He brought his Backs Coach, Clive Griffiths, with him. A lot of hard work was put in but at the end of the day we were unsuccessful, finishing 11th in Mike's first year.

Mike wanted to introduce a new type of play, more advanced with less dependence on forward play and more attractive to watch. But we had a difficult start to the season, going without a win until after Christmas when things picked up and we were back again, beating top teams like Leicester Tigers and Sale Sharks. We also did well in the European Challenge Cup getting to the final and only just losing to Bath.

The next season, 2008/2009, we signed Australian international Chris Latham, although once again things didn't go quite as planned, partly because we had an unbelievable level of injuries. As a result we were down near the bottom once more, although to some extent the injury problem masked the real one – discipline was the big issue. We were giving too many penalties away, didn't kick our own penalties and missed too many chances. We had away victories over Gloucester and Wasps, but we lost to Bourgoin in the semi final of the European Challenge Cup.

17

Relegation

The 2009/2010 season was not a good year for the Warriors either. We had some good times, with wins over Sale Sharks and Newcastle Falcons but the end, playing away to Leeds Carnegie, was bleak. It was Worcester or Leeds who would be relegated. We had to win. We were also aware by then that discipline was a problem, but nevertheless in the first 20 minutes we gave away five soft penalties, conceding twelve easy points to Leeds. We did eventually score the only try and kicked a penalty of our own, but we missed two simple penalties and lost 12–10. The result was our first relegation in 22 years. Even the last game of the season, playing Gloucester at home, had the same inevitability. We played a lot of young players that day. Gloucester had their top team out because if they had won, it was possible they would qualify for the Heineken Cup the following year. It could have been a dream ending after a thrilling game, but then right at the end Willie Walker attempted a relatively simple drop goal – and hit the post. We lost 22–23. Supporters were resigned as they trudged homeward. It was a sad ending to a poor season: we won only three games, but we had drawn four. If we had won just one of those drawn games we would have avoided relegation. Fine margins!

Some of our players had played well, especially the young players, and there was a kind of dogged optimism in the air. But by then Mike Ruddock had resigned. He didn't want a huge pay-off; he's a very modest, honorable and genuinely nice man with a lovely family. In retrospect I think perhaps those very qualities allowed the players to take over and then, without perhaps the leadership they needed, they got confused. We carried out an internal review during which Roger Murray and I spoke to everyone, the coaching staff, the physios, health and fitness team and of course all the players, and asked them for their views. It was great to have Roger alongside me as he had worked with me from the time I first became involved. He had been the President of the old club and his opinion was something I valued very much. Our main question was, how had it happened? It was obvious that there was discontent in the camp, but they had kept it to themselves so the disagreements didn't get aired. We really had lost our way. It had to come down to the Director of Rugby because he hadn't discussed any of these misgivings with me. Perhaps I should have been more interrogative, asked a few more questions. But Mike's attitude had always been that everything would be all right, we were going to win, we were going to win... but we didn't.

Of course it was massively disappointing. But that's sport. In 40 years of business I've had highs and lows. That year there had been more lows than highs, but we all believed we could still make it. We were in a battle, and it was a battle to be won. Sixways was now a state-of-the-art 65 acre site with a 12,060 capacity stadium and plans were in hand to take this up to 20,000. Maybe we made a mistake in 2007 by substituting Mike Ruddock for John Brain. I had felt a change was necessary, but we'll never really know whether that was the right decision. Mike was available and had been very successful in Wales and Ireland. Unfortunately he was not successful at Worcester but was hugely helpful in getting the structure right and blooding many Academy boys.

Following Mike's departure, we became the target for every coach in the world to come to Worcester. I decided then that I would carry out an external review to add to the one we had carried out. We wanted to get right to the heart of what had gone wrong. I involved a company that used the former Harlequins director of rugby, Dean Richards, who had been banned from involvement in the game for three years following the 'bloodgate' scandal in a quarter-final of the Heineken Cup. He was suspended by the European Rugby Cup board, a decision supported by the International Rugby Board, but the precise details of the ban were not clear. Could he do rugby-related consultancy work for us at Worcester? The RFU said yes, he could. That was great news for us because I've always been a great admirer of Dean Richards, both as a player and what he achieved at Leicester and Harlequins. Looking back to when we first got promotion to the Premiership, and he was bundled out of Leicester, I wish I'd gone further in discussions with him about his coming to Worcester. He would have liked to have done so at the time. But I supported the people who had got us promotion. It was loyal, but in retrospect it wasn't the right decision.

Following the review, we took on Richard Hill as Head Coach for the next two years. He had spent the last year working in France but he is one of the most highly qualified and talented coaches in the English game, with a fantastic record in club rugby. He also has a strong belief in developing the right culture off the pitch as well as on. That is exactly what we needed at that time. I was confident Richard would be successful, and the board of directors backed the decision. We did sign some new players ahead of the Championship campaign and retained our young and aspiring players like England Sevens star Jake Abbott and Jonny Arr – Worcester born and bred and connected to the club since they were six years old. Unfortunately we lost Tom Wood, which was disappointing as he had come through our Academy and had become an exceptional player. He has since played for England, which I thought he would do, and naturally I'm delighted. It would, of course, have been even better if he was still playing for Worcester.

We should not have finished twelfth and been relegated. With the players we had we should have finished in the top half of the league. Players like Chris Latham who was towards the end of his career but still a very good player, having played for Australia 78 times; All Blacks Greg Rawlinson, Sammy Tuitupou and Rico Gear; Tongan international Tevita Taumoepeau and their captain Aleki Lutui; Craig Gillies and our captain Pat Sanderson who played for England 16 times; Samoan international Dale Rasmussen, who is a fearless and ferocious tackler; Marcel Garvey, an outstanding winger; and some very good young players like Miles Benjamin; Matt Mullan who has since played for England; Jonny Arr; Joe Carlisle; Jake Abbott; Graham Kitchener; Callum Black; Alex Grove, who played for Scotland; and Tom Wood. There is no doubt that we had the players, but somehow we failed to get them to play as a team.

We did not have any players with a relegation release clause but Chris Latham, Sammy Tuitupou and Rico Gear's contracts were up and, being in the Championship, we did not attempt to re-sign them. We did receive a parachute payment which roughly covered the players' costs, but there were many other costs that had to be covered by the revenue coming into the club via sponsors, ticket sales, etc. which we knew would be considerably down. We budgeted for a loss of £2,000,000 with the intention of returning to the Premiership the following season.

The RFU, in its wisdom, had meanwhile replaced the first past the post principle for promotion from the Championship to the Premiership with a play off system. All the Premiership clubs disagreed with the new format but the RFU knew better. They just did not want to listen, which was particularly frustrating. The format was that there would be twelve clubs in the Championship league instead of 16. Each club would play each other home and away; after 22 games, the top eight clubs would be split into two leagues. Each club would then play each other home and away and after a further six games the top two clubs from each league would play off again. The two semi-finals would be made up of the team winning league A against the runner up in league B and vice versa and that would be a one-off game. The winners would then play one another in a home and away final, while the bottom four clubs would play off to see who would be relegated. The one-off game of the semi final concerned us. However good we were, it was always possible to lose a one-off game, and in addition we would not know for certain whether we were going to be promoted until May 18th. What chance would we have of recruiting for the new Premiership season starting three months later?

The conundrum for any team that has been promoted or for one in the bottom four of the Premiership league is how to break out and become one of the top four sides? We know it is possible; when we were first promoted to the Premiership, Northampton, London Irish and Saracens were often in the bottom four for quite long periods during the season. We also know that Northampton and Harlequins had been relegated during the previous five years. Both these clubs are now among the top four teams and Saracens were runners up in 2010 and won the Premiership Final in 2011. They are, of course, old fashionable clubs with a long history of being at the top.

Worcester has no history of being at the top so it makes it that much more difficult. 2011-2012 was our seventh season in the Premiership and we still have not broken through. We have had three Directors of Rugby/ Head Coach: John Brain, Mike Ruddock and now Richard Hill. All very knowledgeable and very hard working. John Brain, an intelligent man and a great student of forward play, would spend hours getting the scrum and line outs functioning correctly. There was no doubt that this paid off. Worcester had very good line out statistics and were hardly ever out-scrummaged. We were also pretty effective at the break down and the rolling maul. The problem was that our play was limited and too predictable. We survived for three years in the Premiership under John but our highest position had been eighth.

Mike Ruddock and the signing of Chris Latham and the three All Blacks, Sammy Tuitupou, Rico Gear and Greg Rawlinson did not bring success on the pitch but it became obvious that this had lifted the profile of the club in a significant way. Without advertising, we had a deluge of applicants for the job of Director of Rugby/Head Coach, not only from the UK but South Africa, New Zealand and Australia. Some of the people had been successful at both club and international level and we were naturally flattered by the amount of interest. But the reality was that we had been relegated, we were now in the Championship and although we thought, and I still do think, the format was nonsense, we had to accept it was in place. So we had to get on with it. Who could come in and deliver our objective of returning to the Premiership in one year? Not to achieve this would have devastating consequences for the club. Unlike football, the club that is relegated only gets one year's 'parachute money' and if we failed to bounce back we would be significantly less attractive to our sponsors and supporters.

Richard Hill had already achieved success with Bristol, having returned Bristol to the Premiership after they were relegated. He wanted to return to England, having been in France for a year. He had international experience, having played scrum half for England 29 times. He is an ex-school teacher and very knowledgeable about how the game should be played. We were all impressed by his approach and what he had to say. He chose Phil Davies as his forwards coach. Phil is also very experienced, having been with Leeds for a number of years, spent some time with the Welsh Academy and also having played for Wales 46 times as an international.

They both set about organising the pre-season and recruitment of a few players. Recruiting in the summer is not easy as most players have secured contracts but we were fortunate to have a good squad of players, some of whom were from our Academy who we believed would flourish and develop in the Championship.

We set the twin objectives of winning every game in the Championship and developing a number of players. We almost achieved both; we won 30 games out of 31 and the development of players was excellent. In the first 22 games we won 21 games and lost just once to Cornish Pirates at Sixways when we conceded a penalty in the last minute of the game. We still won the league by 20 points but that meant nothing because the top eight clubs in the league were split into two pools of four. We played home and away against London Welsh, Nottingham and Bristol and won all six games, so winning our league was very comfortable. Then came the semi-finals, which was a one-off game only (it has since been changed to home and away). London Welsh were second in our pool so played away to Cornish Pirates, the winners of the other pool and we played Bedford who were second. Of the four semi-finalists, only Worcester met the entry criteria to the Premiership so if we didn't win, no club would be promoted. We had already beaten Bedford twice so the semi-final should not have been a problem, but that was not to be. It turned out to be a dramatic evening with a couple of heart-stopping moments for Worcester supporters. The Chairman of the RFU was at the match and he also knew that if we didn't win it would be extremely embarrassing as he had been party to the new format of the Championship. What a game. Bedford scored a very good try and at half time we were losing by nine points. We played like rabbits caught in the headlights during the first half. Could we come back? We scored three points early in the second half, were playing better and I became more relaxed, thinking we had over 30 minutes to score a try. We came close many times but it was nearly full time before the try came. The match was being televised so I popped inside to see how many minutes were left to play; at the bottom of the screen it showed five minutes 20 seconds yet to play, but as I watched the re-run of the try I saw that it wasn't a try after all. Graham Kitchener had dropped the ball. He had been trying to get nearer to the posts to make the conversion easier because we still needed two points to win the game and in doing so, he was tackled and failed to ground the ball. No try! Five minutes to go. Kai Horstman picked the ball up at the back of the scrum and crashed over the line from about six metres and Joe Carlisle stepped up and coolly kicked the ball between the posts. Seven points; we could breath again, we had won the match. Then came a second heart-stopping moment. There were still one and a half minutes left to play, so there was time for the restart. We had to make sure we didn't give a penalty away. Bedford re-started, we caught the ball and moved up the field towards the touch line when, for some inexplicable reason, the referee awarded Bedford a penalty. It was too far out for their kicker so he kicked the ball into touch. They won the lineout and worked the ball towards our goal line. They attempted a drop goal, but it was well wide. It was now full time, we had won the match. But had we? There was now a minute or so (it seemed much longer at the time)... utter confusion. After the drop goal attempt a Bedford player ran forward, caught the ball from the re-bound, grounded it and claimed a try. Fortunately the recording on TV showed that the ball had gone out over the dead ball line and then bounced back into play. We had finally won the match. The feeling of celebration and relief was palpable. The bars stayed open until the early hours. It was yet another match at Sixways that I, and every Warriors supporter, will never forget.

Looking back, I can only think that the occasion had got to our players whereas the Bedford players really had nothing to gain really apart from spoiling the party for Worcester. They had some good players and we knew we could have lost on that particular day. If we were to play Bedford a hundred times, we would probably lose on at least one occasion. All year people had been talking about that one-off semi-final game. On the day, a much superior team can get it wrong. There have been many giant killing days in the football FA Cup, indeed not long after I first arrived in Worcester, Worcester City beat Liverpool in the FA Cup in 1959.

We then played Cornish Pirates in a home and away final. We chose to play the away game first, which we won 21-12. The Pirates had some very good players and again, like Bedford, played with complete freedom as they too had nothing to lose. They could not be promoted while we had everything to lose. We took a nine point lead into the final game which was played at Sixways. The match was televised and we had a sell-out crowd of just over 12,000. It was a lovely Spring evening and the atmosphere was electric. We were never behind but the Pirates kept coming and they never gave up. We won on the evening 25-20 (46-32 on aggregate). Another great match at Sixways and this time without the drama of the Bedford game. We were now back in the Premiership. Richard Hill, Phil Davies and the players, with a very good support team, had been magnificent throughout and deserved success. It was also great for our fans who had supported the Warriors through thick and thin, whatever the weather, both at home and away.

The Championship format is, to put it mildly, a ridiculous structure that does not and never will work, and must be changed. The previous management of the RFU compared it with deciding the winner of the Premiership, but I have tried to explain to them that although a lot of people don't agree with the play-off system in the Premiership, we have been able to sell it to our supporters because top clubs are often without their international players – there are ten or even eleven international weekends, six or seven of which the Premiership teams have to play through – and the play-off gives them a chance to redress the balance when they have all their players back at the end of the season. There is still an anomaly, because it is possible for a team to be top of the Premiership before the play-offs and still not be in the final at Twickenham – a lot of rugby people have difficulty with this – but at least there is a reason for it, since many of the clubs have played under strength due to players playing for England. In the Championship there are no international players, so there is no reason for a play-off system, and the comparison with the Premiership is complete nonsense. In any case, the difference between being the losing finalist at Twickenham is that even if you lose, you're still in the Premiership and still pretty well off because you've had a good crowd with a good share of the gate. In the case of the Championship, it could cost a club millions because they haven't been promoted even though they are clearly the best team.

RELEGATION

Bristol comfortably won the 2011/2012 Championship League after 22 games, having played all the other teams, both home and away. But they lost to Cornish Pirates in the semi-final of the play-offs. London Welsh beat Bedford in the other semi-final, so the final was London Welsh v Cornish Pirates. It was generally thought that out of the four semi-finalists only Bristol met the entry criteria for the Premiership. This was then challenged by London Welsh but the RFU ruled that neither finalist met the criteria and London Welsh were informed of this decision before the final was played. London Welsh won the final and immediately appealed against the decision.

In the meantime Newcastle, who finished bottom of the Premiership, thought they had been given a reprieve. Instead of being relegated they would be back in the Premiership for the next season (2012/2013). If there was no promotion, there would be no relegation, but would that be the case?

The Championship final was on the 30th May and the appeal was eventually upheld more than four weeks later. London Welsh were promoted and Newcastle were finally relegated. This process must have been agonising for everybody involved, for both Newcastle and London Welsh.

It is just another reason why the format of the Championship was ill conceived. It was never thought through and only came about because the RFU wanted to reduce the size of the league from 16 to 12 clubs for financial reasons. What they hadn't taken into account was the clubs would now have 22 instead of 30 games to play, making it difficult for them to survive financially. Surprisingly, the RFU did not consult any Premiership clubs before they reduced the league to twelve clubs. Equally surprising was that Rob Andrew could not see that a twelve club league would not work without cobbling together the ridiculous play-off system. Rob Andrew was Head of Elite Rugby at the time, had played in the professional era and had been Director of Rugby at Newcastle for a number of years. He must have known the Championship with twelve teams would not work. I have often wondered whether anyone at the time was listening to him?

The RFU have introduced changes to the Championship structure in each of the three years since it was introduced in 2009, the latest eliminating the play-offs except for the top four clubs, so it would appear that the other eight clubs will not have enough games. The tinkering goes on. Why don't the RFU scrap the play-off structure and go to a 14 club league with the club that finishes top after 26 games being the champions? I just do not understand; it is such a simple solution.

Francis Baron was Chief Executive of the RFU and Martyn Thomas was Chairman at the time, and both were at the centre of the process of formulating the new structure of the Championship. They were also in charge when Martin Johnson was appointed head coach for England. Both decisions have proved to be disappointing. Martin Johnson was a great player and a very good captain but had no experience of managing or coaching a rugby team at any level. It was a huge gamble and sadly it did not pay off. The unintended consequences of those two decisions have been detrimental to the growth and well-being of English rugby

It is interesting now to compare that process with the way the new Chief Executive, Ian Ritchie, conducted the process of appointing Stuart Lancaster to be the new England Head Coach. Ian invited and had many discussions with a number of very experienced senior rugby people including Rob Andrew before making his decision.

It has been obvious to me for some time that both the Premiership and the Championship should be made up of 14 teams. The Premiership teams should have a three year franchise similar to the way rugby league operates. This would produce many advantages:

1. It would enable clubs to have the freedom to develop their academy players because they would be relieved of the fear of relegation.
2. It would also encourage clubs to play attacking rugby instead of a negative 'we must not lose' approach.
3. It would give our supporters four more Premiership games which they prefer to watch.
4. It would ensure greater financial stability.
5. It would allow second tier rugby in England (the Championship teams) time to develop their grounds, their infrastructure and their crowd support. If a club cannot build a support base of 10,000 it will not be able to be independently viable.

Being able to plan for three years would also be financially beneficial for the clubs because young developing players cost a lot less than overseas players. The other very important factor is that this would benefit the English national side. We have seen how this approach has benefited the Spanish football team who have won the World Cup, Olympic Gold and now the European Cup. Spain did not produce one of the greatest teams in the history of the game without a radical rethink. If we are to be successful we also have to change.

RELEGATION

The RFU is essentially composed of amateur clubs – 'constituent bodies', or CBs, including counties, Oxford and Cambridge, the Army, RAF and Navy and the England Schools Rugby Football Union. Each CB annually elects one member to the RFU council. Unfortunately none of the people involved in it have ever run a professional team. They make decisions on the hoof and don't understand professional rugby or the financial implications. The structure of the RFU is totally inadequate and inappropriate to deal with professional rugby. I am hopeful that the debacle of England's performance, both on and off the field, at the World Cup in New Zealand in 2011 will act as a catalyst for change. The new Chief Executive, Ian Ritchie; new Head Coach, Stuart Lancaster, and new Chairman, Bill Beaumont, looks like a very strong team.

It was mid-May 2011 by the time we had gained promotion back to the Premiership so we had no time to lose. I asked Richard Hill to prepare a list of what he required so that we would be successful the following season. It was a relatively short shopping list: number one was a defence coach. I told Richard he needed to look no further than Phil Larder, if he was available.

When the players reported for pre-season training in the summer of 2011, our most senior player, Pat Sanderson, announced that he had been advised to retire because of injury. Pat had been a wonderful player and a great captain. He had captained Worcester for our first six years in the Premiership during which time he had played and captained England. He is very knowledgeable about how the game should be played and his retirement left a massive hole in our squad. It was a major set-back.

Richard Hill, or 'Hilly' as he is known, requested four new players to give us more strength in depth, a pre-season training camp in Geneva and some additional equipment for the gym. He was very happy with the back up team of Ben MacDonald, Head of Medical Services; Mike Lancaster, Senior Physiotherapist; Stuart Pickering, Head of Strength & Conditioning, and Alun Carter, Team Manager. The back up team play a vital role in preparing and organising the players so they can play to their maximum ability for a full 80 minutes in any weather conditions. It is equally vital when players are injured that they return to full fitness in the shortest possible time. Rugby is a very physical game and the players take a lot of knocks and bumps so they need to be regularly fine tuned. To help in this process, each game and training session is videoed and analysed by Tom Tench, our Performance Analyst. In addition each player has a heart monitor attached to himself so that his level of effort can be observed and recorded by Kyle Goggin, our Sports Scientist. To play rugby at Premiership level the players have to be extremely fit. They spend a lot of time in the gym and on the training ground so it is also very important to have the right diet with the correct nutritional value. To ensure our players achieve optimum results we employ a top nutritionalist and we have a dedicated chef to prepare their food. The players do not have all the meals at the club so they are given details of what they should eat. They are then tested for body fat on a regular basis.

Global Positioning System (GPS) technology was used at the club for the first time in the 2011/2012 season to analyse match demands on players and help manage the training load. The technology is based on that which might be found in a car. Players wear a small mobile phone-size unit that sits in a vest just above the shoulder blades, on the lower neck. Each unit houses a GPS chip, which allows the sports scientists to see how far a player has travelled in a match. This of course varies depending on position (front row forwards 5.5km; scrum half 7.5km), but the distances players travel at various speeds and the metres they cover per minute are also calculated, allowing the support team to assess how hard the players are working regardless of how long they are on the field.

In addition to GPS, heart rate monitoring is collected in real time to evaluate how much stress a player is under. This is used to evaluate how well a player deals with a given amount of work in a match or training, and also gives the support team the ability to review training intensity and establish whether a particular session has produced the desired intensity. These intensity measures collected via GPS and heart rate are evaluated next to a player's match contributions, and the effectiveness of the contributions. These four factors are then used to as a marker of match fitness. For example a hooker who covers 74 metres per minute (the average is 65), makes 60 contributions (45 average) with an effectiveness of 90% and 55 minutes above 85% max heart rate (40 minutes is average) would be considered fit and effective, because while his heart rate is above average, his contributions, distance per minute and effectiveness are high. This would suggest that his high heart rate response is due to the amount of work he is doing (he is doing well with 90% effectiveness). In addition to a GPS chip, each unit contains an accelerometer. This collects force measurements from every movement a player is involved in, from walking to running, running to sprinting, or scrum-engaged to making a tackle. Every aspect of a match involves a player producing or absorbing force. Force production and its absorption results in tissue damage which can take up to five days to recover fully from. By knowing how many impacts and how hard those impacts are, the support team can adjust an individual's recovery and work at the start of a week to maximise recovery and ensure he is in top shape for the weekend.

This technology is at an early stage of development but these examples show how it is already impacting on training and evaluating match performance. As technology evolves the monitoring units get ever smaller; the mobile phone-size units currently used will soon be the size of a micro chip. The National Rugby League in Australia has already begun experimenting in using GPS inside match balls! The RFU has one year left on a PhD study before the IRB will pass external units used in all rugby competitions, and it won't be long before every player's GPS data is being sent to our TV screens at home.

The computer software that is now available is very sophisticated and enables the players to analyse their own performance. Equally important is the information that is produced and dissected by Tom Tench, our Performance Analyst, so that our coaches know which players are performing and which are not. They will then talk to the players concerned about how they can improve. Sometimes a player is replaced in the team so that he can concentrate on improving a particular skill. It is all very professional and very well organised by Richard Hill. Indeed, it is difficult to imagine the extent of the work, effort and resource that goes into the preparation of the team for every game we play. Richard, with Phil Larder and Nigel Redman, will also study a number of games of the team we are due to play next, looking for any weaknesses and their style of play so they can come up with a winning game plan. With this level of preparation, some supporters watching our games must be thinking 'why does it go wrong?' Richard Hill and his colleagues tell me, "It's the red mist that comes down".

The question then is: "Are our players good enough; are they fit enough and can the coaches develop them into a cohesive, disciplined winning team?" That is the challenge for the players, the coaches and the back-up staff. The Premiership is made up of twelve teams. One club will be relegated. What we have to ensure is that it isn't Worcester.

Worcester Warriors made progress on the field, and off the field the stadium and the surrounding facilities have been transformed beyond recognition. Back in 1992, when I first became involved, there were three pitches and a small clubhouse with 28 acres of land. We now have 65 acres of land, eight full size pitches (three floodlit) and many small pitches, a very substantial clubhouse and a stadium that currently has a capacity of over 12,000 which we plan to increase to 20,000 in due course. There is also a new access road and car parking for 1,250 cars. The big indoor training centre is unique to Worcester and is often used when the weather is inclement. We can provide up to 1,500 hot meals for our supporters on match days and on non-match days the facilities are used for conferences, meetings, dinners, exhibitions and many other activities. We also have a licence for marriages at Sixways. The David Lloyd Centre will have three indoor and six outdoor tennis courts, an indoor and an outdoor swimming pool, a full gymnasium and a café. A hotel is also planned making Sixways a significant complex and one of the top rugby clubs in England.

On the professional rugby side there are 35 Warrior players, 15 Academy players with a back up team of 20 in total, including coaches, physios, strength and conditioning, analyst, team manager, team doctor, etc. On the amateur side, there are over 500 mini juniors, four senior male teams and two ladies teams with four players in the England team. No other club combines such a significant amateur club with a Premiership team, making Worcester unique..

We have come a long way. Our Academy has produced four English players, one Scottish international and over 20 Premiership players. We have turned Worcester into a rugby city. What we haven't yet achieved is winning the Premiership and then going on to win the Heineken Cup. That is our ambition and when we have achieved that we will want to do it again. Is that too ambitious? I don't think so. Will we achieve it? We will have to wait and see. It might be worth a small investment at Ladbrookes.

18

Looking Ahead

When I sold my shares in Worcester Heat Systems to Bosch in 1996, I suppose I could have bought a yacht or become a tax exile. But that isn't the way I saw it. It wasn't like winning the lottery: I'd gone from being broke to becoming reasonably well off and then very, very well off - and I'd gathered a few toys on the way. I'm very fond of my Aston Martin DB9 and Beatrice and I enjoy travelling. But we still live in the house we bought in the village of Kempsey, just south of Worcester, some 40 years ago. We've extended it, of course, but I wouldn't change it. I can look across the lawn to the Malverns in the distance, and I like to see the ducks flying in and out and the heron by the pond, even if it does take the odd fish. Besides, a lot of other people helped me to earn that money and I wanted to do something with it, something worthwhile for the people of Worcester who had helped me create my wealth.

Well before I sold the company I had agreed to become chairman of Worcester Community Health Trust, partly because I believed this was a way I could put something back into the city that had become my home, but also because I had a personal reason for being interested in the NHS. When my son Mark was born we discovered he had a condition called hydrocephalus – 'water on the brain'. I had just started the business and although I usually managed to get home for lunch, Beatrice bore most of the burden. Mark had a major operation when he was six months old and although he still has some slight disability, he is a successful young man, able to work and drive his beloved car and enjoy life.

That experience perhaps made me more aware of how difficult life could be for parents with sick children. A few years later I was confronted with just how desperate their plight could be. It was my daughter Jill's school friend who visited our house many times and who was now trying to cope with three young children, one of whom was life-limited and required 24 hour care. This young mother was exhausted. She had heard of a children's hospice in Birmingham which provided some of the help she needed. Acorns had been opened in Selly Oak in 1988 to provide not only respite care and a place where children and their families could find real comfort and care, but also outreach services to help families at home. I said I didn't know if I could do anything, but I'd have a look at Acorns and see if something like it might be possible in Worcester. When I visited the Birmingham Acorns I was overwhelmed by the work being done there. It was an impressive place: not just the specially designed building and facilities, but the compassion of the staff created such a positive atmosphere.

I said to John Overton, the Acorns chief executive, "Why don't we have one of these in Worcester?" He said they'd love to, but they couldn't afford it; they had plans to expand, but they were having difficulty in simply supporting the existing hospice. So I said I'd be interested in them doing a survey to see if there was a need for a hospice in Worcester, and if Acorns could handle it. There was – and it could.

First of all we had to find a site for the new hospice. My old solicitor friend, David Hallmark, found one. An elderly couple called Willie and June Sayce owned three acres of land on the Bath Road coming into Worcester and where for some 40 years they had run a smallholding with some cattle, poultry and donkeys. They had been approached many times over the years to sell the land for development, but they had always resisted, unhappy for it simply to be built on. David explained the idea for Acorns to them, and they decided that this, at last, was the answer. The site was worth well over a million pounds but they sold it for a very much reduced price to Acorns. Although Mr Sayce died soon afterwards, his widow said he had been happy to know that they had done something to help the children. The only proviso was that the two donkeys should remain on the land – so we built them a stable. June Sayce is still very much alive and takes a great interest in the progress of Acorns.

Fund-raising started in earnest after that. I got the ball rolling with a £1,000,000 donation. I declined the post of chairman but was much involved in the fund raising and asked Sir Michael Perry, a friend of mine who had recently retired as Chairman of Unilever, to take on the role. Our goal was £4 million. And we achieved it. Acorns in Worcester now provides care for life-limited children and their families throughout Worcestershire, Herefordshire and Gloucestershire. Michael did an excellent job.

Of course I get the Warriors involved too. We carry the Acorns logo on all our training kit and we donate £1 from every item with the logo sold in our Sixways Store. The players are also very keen to help directly, both with fund-raising and visiting the hospice. A couple of Christmases ago we ran a competition in schools to design an Acorns shirt for our Christmas game and then we auctioned the shirts off afterwards and gave the proceeds to Acorns. I don't give the financial handouts I did in the early days, but we do continue to lift its profile so that people are always aware of it. Randy Lerner, the American owner of Aston Villa, was so impressed with our involvement, that he put Acorns on their players' shirts for a couple of years, and Acorns is now Villa's charity partner.

Acorns now gets some money from Government and is substantially supported by its charity shops, public donations, endowments and so on. But the number of beds in the hospice is limited, and much of its work involves going out into the community. The need is always increasing, and so too is the need for funding. These life-limited children often need 24 hour care, seven days a week. As they are now better cared for, they are living longer; whereas once they were expected to die before 19, they now survive. It is a real and heartbreaking problem for parents who look after them.

When the Worcester Acorns opened March 2005, life in retirement was already proving pretty busy. I had established the Duckworth Worcestershire Trust in 1998 whose aim was to conserve, protect and enhance Worcestershire's natural and urban environments, and at the same time help disadvantaged people such as those with special needs or who had difficulty in finding employment, particularly if they had become involved in minor crime. That was the fundamental aim, but of course within that all kinds of projects could be set up and managed, often in partnership with Worcester City Council or the County Council. At the outset I got involved with several capital projects such as installing a CCTV system for Worcester, to which the Duckworth Trust was a major contributor. We also helped with lighting and conserving Edgar Tower, the fountains by the river, and the restoration of Fish Street. Not only was I able to give something back to my adopted city in this way, but I suppose it fitted my basic philosophy to make Worcester a better place to live.

I rather believe in what President Kennedy said: 'Ask not what your country can do for you - ask what you can do for your country'. There is sometimes a rather pedestrian feeling in this country that 'I pay my taxes, so I expect the state to look after me'. And on the whole it will: it works. But we can help to make it better than that. The state reaches a certain standard, but the local community can take it higher. And that means anything from picking up litter to acquiring and conserving land or buildings. If we throw away an empty takeaway box or a beer can, someone will have to pick it up and dispose of it. Apart from anything else, that's a wasted resource. People can be prosecuted – using CCTV – and maybe they will eventually learn, but you can also try to engage with people, with communities, encouraging them to want things to look better, to be better. I suppose David Cameron's Big Society is essentially about the same thing – he has given it a higher profile. One naturally hopes all politicians will back it, but inevitably politics can be divisive because if an idea is introduced by one party the others oppose it.

Buying Chapter Meadows to safeguard its future was one of the first projects of the Duckworth Trust. In 1998 the Diocese of Worcester wanted to sell the 35 acres of meadowland that border the River Severn. For centuries these watery acres had been managed by the Romans, Norman monks and more recently by Worcester Cathedral. Winter floods were followed by haymaking in early summer, the pastures then grazed by cattle. The pattern continues today, now under the management of Worcester City Council and the Worcestershire Wildlife Trust, together with the work of the Duckworth Trust environmental wardens and a host of volunteers. The new Diglis Bridge has provided the final link in the path along the riverbank and Chapter Meadows so that everyone can now enjoy this ancient and beautiful landscape with its perfect harmony of man and nature, a cricket ball's hit from the Worcestershire County Cricket Club's ground at New Road and the Cathedral.

The environmental wardens were very much part of the early days of the Duckworth Trust when we concentrated on litter, fly tipping and graffiti. The volunteer litter warden scheme was set up in 2000 and there are now over 100 such volunteers in Worcester and Malvern, acting as the eyes and ears for the Trust, organising their own events or taking part in the annual Rubbish? Sort It! campaign which encourages communities to clean up and recycle rubbish within their own areas. We work closely with community groups and schools, and in 2004 the Trust took on the management of the Worcester Scrap House Project; it is now the Worcestershire Resource Exchange (WRE) housed in an old brick factory building on the Shrub Hill industrial estate.

I find the WRE a really stimulating place. A huge tree made from cardboard, metal, buttons, fabric, plastic and old paint tins spreads its branches in the entrance, so one can begin to get an idea of the creativity within. It's an Aladdin's cavern of treasure trove, full of everything from barrels of glass lenses to piles of felt, from fabrics to industrial scrap, cardboard, buttons, plastic, part of a wider network of over 100 'scrapstores' throughout the country, linked through the charity Scrapstore UK. I'm endlessly fascinated by what the manager, Beth Holland, and her colleagues together with some 20 volunteers, create out of what would otherwise simply be thrown into landfill. About 75 local companies contribute their waste to the scheme.

As Beth Holland explains: "People join the WRE as members. We've got families, schools, students and individuals, about 1,120 in all, and we have opportunities for training, volunteering, work for students and people from disadvantaged backgrounds. They can take whatever they like from the WRE, and we price by trolley capacity. You can squash as much as you like in to your shopping trolley and pay about £13.50 for a full one, with negotiation for anything too big to fit in. Then we always ask people what they're going to do with the stuff. Sometimes they're artists, or teachers or parents with ideas for children, or they're children with vivid imaginations, or older people who enjoy crafts and just making things. We make our own items to sell, like packs for making your own toys or household products. Sometimes we get a few pallets of Farrow and Ball paint – elbows out for that!" As soon as the information is put on the WRE website it's all gone in 48 hours.

The WRE is open on Thursday, Fridays and Saturdays, and it is a real expression of what the Trust is all about. It doesn't just recycle or re-use what most people would call rubbish, it somehow engenders a real enthusiasm for managing waste as a whole, raising awareness among companies and people about what can be achieved; and it engages not only the young and the old but those who find it hard to cope with the world because of some difficulty or disadvantage.

Then in 2004 we opened the Pump House Environment Centre in Gheluvelt Park, that sweep of green space where the Barbourne Brook runs down to the River Severn. I've always been fond of this park. For those who don't know Worcester, I suppose it is quite a hidden place, not on anybody's tourist route, although the walking or cycling route from the centre of the City past Pitchcroft and the racecourse by the river is a fine way to get there. It was created in 1922 to commemorate the Battle of Gheluvelt in Belgium in 1914, where the 2nd Battalion of the Worcestershire Regiment fought with such courage and determination that they prevented the advancing German army from taking control of the Channel ports. There is now a new memorial to depict the battle; it actually looks as though a bomb's hit it, as if there's been an explosion resulting in a lot of rusty metal. At first glance it looks like something you might want to get rid of, not actually create. However, once you understand its meaning, it works.

The Duckworth Trust became involved in updating and improving Gheluvelt Park and received a large grant from the Heritage Lottery scheme. Refurbishment included extending the park, replacing an old paddling pool with a 'splash pad' and installing outdoor gym equipment. These improvements included the Pump House. I had always liked the look of it. It was brick built, gabled, with a distinctive, decorative Victorian sense of its own importance in 1858 by a great water engineer, Thomas Hawkesley, as part of the improvements to Worcester's water supply. There had been several outbreaks of cholera in the city, blamed chiefly on the water from the River Severn. Although Severn Trent Water still occupied a small part of the Pump House, the building had been neglected for a long time. I had the idea for an environment centre...

So in August, 2004, the Pump House Environment Centre was formally opened. Nick Owen from BBC *Midlands Today* joined me for the opening ceremony. Its mission was to raise community awareness of environmental issues, give information and advice and stimulate new ideas about how people might improve things. We used the opportunity of restoring the building to demonstrate just how sustainable materials and technologies could be used: rainwater harvesting, ground source heat pumps, solar energy and sheep's wool insulation. We installed insulated pipes for hot water supply throughout the building, under floor heating systems and small-scale wind turbines. The flooring was Marmoleum, made from linseed oil and jute among other things; we used natural paints, sisal carpets and natural clay plaster. It's now the home of the Trust, with a large meeting room and all facilities and a flourishing café open seven days a week, and has been visited by both David Cameron and Robin Walker.

That same year I was awarded the OBE for 'services to the community, especially the environment and sport in Worcestershire'. My investiture was a great occasion. Beatrice, Mark, Jill and I arrived in style at Buckingham Palace, excited that we were firstly going inside the palace and then meeting the Queen. It was a lovely sunny day and we were allowed to drive through the gates right up to the steps of the palace. Inside we were directed into a reception room via a massive hall with an array of pictures and chandeliers.

It was truly magnificent. The officials were friendly and helpful. We were then invited to have a drink and mingle with the other recipients and their families. There were about 60 of us receiving awards and we were directed to another room for a briefing. The Queen's Equerry, dressed in uniform complete with ceremonial sword, explained how to address the Queen and how the ceremony would be conducted. Again, it was another magnificent room. The families sat in front of where the Queen stood. I could clearly see Beatrice, Mark and Jill and then my name was called. I went forward, bowed and the Queen greeted me and gave me my award. She then spoke to me about what I had done regarding the environment and sport. Jill later said the Queen smiled when I was talking to her: "What did you say?" I said I told the Queen that I'd like to take on the job of keeping the Palace clean. I didn't let on for about a week, but after Beatrice had told everybody what I'd said to the Queen, I admitted I hadn't really said that. It was a great and memorable day; we had our photograph taken and then we went for lunch in Harry's Bar in South Audley Street.

Another great occasion for me was when I was made a Freeman of the City of Worcester in 2008. Worcester is my adopted city and where I built my business with the help of its people, and I have tried to give something back to the city that has been my home, my work, and my life, for the past 50 years. It was very flattering to think I am only the 29th person to receive the honour, the first being Lord Nelson in 1803; later recipients have included Stanley Baldwin, Edward Elgar, Winston Churchill and my old friend Lord (Peter) Walker.

Receiving the OBE and being given the Freedom of the City of Worcester fills me with great pride and I am overwhelmed that I should have been considered for these awards, which I was delighted to accept.

Being successful in my business life has given me a lot of satisfaction in being able to bring Acorns to Worcester, to run the Duckworth Worcestershire Trust and establish Premiership rugby in Worcester. My old team at Bosch have carried on where I left off. The company continues to grow and their Chief Executive Officer, Richard Soper, received the CBE before moving on to run the Bosch North American Heating operation. Carl Arntzen, who we took on as a trainee engineer, now heads up the company in Worcester and I'm confident that he will be very successful.

We have to encourage young bright people to work in manufacturing and realise just how exciting and rewarding it can be. We need to produce world quality products so that British people will buy them. This would then benefit our balance of payments, making us all better off. If we don't produce the right products it will result in us not having the luxury of choice of buying foreign products because we will not be able to afford them. We will not be able to pay our way in the world and the British pound will be devalued. I am still optimistic that we will be successful. We have a lot of talented people in this country. The Prime Minister, David Cameron, and the Chancellor, George Osborne, now realise the importance of manufacturing.

Locally it would be great if Bosch went ahead with their plans to build a new factory. Worcester is becoming a growth city. The University has increased its student population from 5,000 to over 10,000 and we are fortunate to have Professor David Green, the Chief Executive and Vice Chancellor and the principal driver of the expansion of the University. The main campus, once on the edge of the city, has now spread nearer the city centre. There are now student accommodation blocks and a new sports hall which will be the first of its kind, designed for wheelchair sport and with a capacity of 2,000 spectators. But the most exciting development is a new £60 million library, opened by the Queen in July 2012 – Jubilee Year. It is a stunning new building both externally and internally called The Hive, situated next to the racecourse. I met the Queen and the Duke of Edinburgh at the opening and later for lunch in the Guildhall. Being a Deputy Lieutenant and a Freeman of the city, I was asked to sit next to the Queen. It was a wonderful occasion and one I will never forget.

The Warriors are continuing to help Acorns through our partnership agreement. Last year the club contributed over £108,000 and plans to do more in future. Acorns is doing a magnificent job with the help of over 100 volunteers and making such a difference to lots of families.

Our own family life has changed in recent years. In June 2007, Evie, our granddaughter, was born and life has changed for the better. I'm now bang up to-date with *Peppa Pig*, *Tom and Jerry* and *Madeline*. Evie is such fun and we all love her to bits. She is time-consuming but fascinating and has taken over our lives. We love it.

The Duckworth Trust continues with its work and hopefully we will soon see Worcester voted Britain's cleanest city. It is a battle to contain graffiti and rubbish. What I do find extraordinary is how often people, even professionals, drive off the motorway and throw their plastic coffee cup through the car window at the first roundabout. The amount of rubbish thrown out of car windows is unbelievable. Can the Duckworth Trust change this? It will take time unfortunately, but we can hope.

At Sixways we now have a much more extensive coaching team for the 2012/2013 season. Phil Davies has been replaced by Nigel Redman; Phil Vickery has joined us as scrum coach, and Mathieu Rourre as our new attack coach. Together with head coach Richard Hill and the proven ability of defence coach, Phil Larder, they will I believe make a formidable team.

Over the last few years I've spent a lot of time building for the future. I've been able to attract a significant new investor who is a real rugby man and is always positive and it is just fantastic to have his support. We have also built a very strong board of directors; so much so that I can now relax and become the non-executive chairman. I believe we have built something very special at Sixways and I'm optimistic we will be successful both on and off the field.

Worcester has become a great place to live or visit and I'm pleased I've been able to play a small part in its development. What would make it even more exciting would be the Warriors winning the Premiership and the Heineken Cup. Bosch is a great company but it's just a pity they don't do rugby: if they did, we would probably be the finest rugby club in the world. The 2012-2013 season is our eighth year in the Premiership. I believe we can start to move forward. We will have to wait and see!! I've checked the depth of the garage and it still can hold the latest Rolls Royce.

Acknowledgements

I would like to thank three people who have helped me write this book. Firstly, Diana Winsor who spent many hours with me; without her enthusiasm and guidance I would not have been able to complete the first draft. Secondly, Louise Brook, my ever dedicated and supportive Personal Assistant for the past 20 years, who has cheerfully done most of the typing and hard work. And thirdly, my wife Beatrice for her help and encouragement – and, of course, for the £300 (£4,500 in today's money) she gave me all those years ago that enabled me to set up the business. It would not have been possible for me to be successful without her support over the 50 years I've been involved with industry and rugby.

I would also like to record my deep gratitude to the late Peter Walker (later Lord Walker) for his support, advice and friendship over many years.

Finally I would like to thank Colonel Cronin, Vic Carter and Ted Farrell, three very good bankers; and my fellow directors: Nigel Collis, Arthur Money, Roger Tomlinson, David Jones, David Steade, Kevin Lee and Richard Soper. With their help, together with all our employees, we built a very successful company. Bosch, one of the world's finest companies, is now taking the company forward. Without the success of the company I started in 1962 I would not have been able to bring Premiership Rugby or Acorns to Worcester. Nor would I have been able to create the Duckworth Worcestershire Trust.

Index

INDEX